D1233333

Whatever is written on job enrichment, behavioural science or employee motivation is usually long winded and academic, or else simple truisms, such as 'a happy worker is a good worker'. In both cases managers, not surprisingly, respond with scepticism and the self assurance that in practice things are considerably different.

But here, for the first time, is evidence that the theories do work, that truisms can be applied. From her studies and investigations the author has brought together actual cases where attention to the motivation of employees of many types in firms of different sizes and pursuits in the United Kingdom and Europe has brought about job enrichment with obvious benefits to productivity, labour turnover and relations between employers and employees. The cases will be an invaluable guide to application for all who see the logic of job enrichment, and an eye opener for sceptics.

contents

NOT
FOR BREAD ALONE

an appreciation of job enrichment

NOT
FOR BREAD ALONE

an appreciation of job enrichment

Lynda King Taylor

London

BUSINESS BOOKS LIMITED

First published 1972
2nd Edition 1973

© LYNDA KING TAYLOR 1972

ISBN 0 220 66233 9

This book has been set in 10 on 11pt. Imprint
and printed by Lowe & Brydone (Printers) Ltd., Haverhill, Suffolk
for the publishers Business Books Limited
(registered office: 110 Fleet Street, London, E.C.4),
publishing offices: Mercury House, Waterloo Road, London, S.E.1.

Made and printed in Great Britain

contents

foreword

From the days of the Industrial Revolution nearly a century and a half ago, there has been a fantastic change in the relationship between those who manage and those who are managed. Management which was vested in ownership has given way to professional management on behalf of owners who are never seen, except for the sprinkling that attend the shareholders' annual meeting. The management is largely self-perpetuating and senior management with a seat on the board is very often a man's lifetime ambition realised.

The workers have risen from completely unorganised groups cruelly exploited and persecuted to strong trade union organisation recognised as the third estate of the realm. Worker–management relations have developed in many varied ways, all with the objective in these later post-war years to secure the personal involvement of men at work in the managerial problems of the enterprise with the maximising of profitability and the right to have a say in the sharing of those profits.

At least that is the bare bones of the theory and certainly modern management with whom I am in daily contact are much more concerned about the well-being of their labour force than making undue distribution of profits to the shareholders. The philosophy is a fair return on the capital invested for its use and after that plough back into the company and its people.

Technological development has taken a lot of the personal pleasure that a craftsman experienced in his job away from him. A working environment good enough half a century ago is not acceptable today. Being told what to do but not why it is to be done and what the ultimate result will be in a personal sense to the worker is no longer acceptable to management or workers.

Foreword

Millions of words have been written on the subject of industrial relations. A great number of people, the leaders of the workers and the leaders of management, have spent countless hours together and separately trying to find the perfect formula, to seek the one way in which complete co-operation and harmony can be secured, a method by which strikes and lock-out could be ruthlessly discarded and made as redundant as the penny-farthing bicycle has been as a means of transport.

So far all such efforts have failed in their main purpose, but people of goodwill in industry persevere and there is no doubt that one day success will come. To the cynics who doubt this, believing the task to be too great and the obstacles too big to overcome, I can only ask who would have thought that one day there really would be a man on the moon?

A field of enquiry and research that has not been very fully explored is the environment of men at work and its impact upon him as an individual.

This book repairs that omission dealing as it does in a non-academic way with employee motivation and involving successful job enrichment programmes. The case studies are fascinatingly clear from home and abroad and show the benefits that can come to management and employee alike by a recognition that people matter and it is essentially a part of management's task to see that they count.

October 1971   LORD ROBENS
London

list of illustrations

acknowledgements

Now I would like to thank various people while absolving them from any responsibility for what I have written. It is more than difficult to acknowledge all those who have helped me with this book and unfortunately too many to mention all by name, though they may recognise some of the points they made, particularly in the case studies.

There are those who gave me much encouragement and time to follow my own interests, and in particular I would like to single out the Industrial Society, in London; John Garnett, its director, and Bryan Stevens, Assistant Director.

There are those whose companies appear in this book, and who spared me considerable time in discussing specific problems, many whose indebtedness I have included at the commencement of the studies.

There are those who provided inspiration, when lacking, and though they may not agree or approve with all I have written their suggestions and criticisms, like their inspiration, have proved invaluable. In particular, Professor Frederick Herzberg of Case Western University in Ohio; Dr William Paul, Director in North Paul Associates, London; Saul Gellerman, President Gellerman Kay Corp., New Jersey, USA and Irene Innes, Industrial Relations Adviser and Alex Irvine, Associate Adviser—both of the Industrial Society, London; Michael Tebay once of the British Aircraft Corpn. now lost to the School of Business Studies, Harvard University, USA; Graham Cleverley who was Manpower Director at International Publishing Corp. and George Sivewright, Chief Training Officer at the Shipbuilding ITB, Dr John Adair, Assistant Director, Industrial Society, London and Research Fellow at Jesus College, Oxford; Robert Ardrey who with kind

Acknowledgements

permission from his publishers, Collins, allowed me to quote from his book *The Territorial Imperative* when I was in search of a conclusion.

The Mayor of Bellapais in Cyprus provided me with peace and quiet in order that the book could be thought out, and his villagers tolerated the noise of the typewriter in the early hours of the morning.

There are those along with my publisher Alan Reid who provided helpful editorial criticism, in particular Richard Oldcorn, Director, Foote, Cone & Belding Ltd., London and Prunella Bell at Cadbury-Schweppes, London. A great source of patience, coffee and final draft typing proved to be Amelia Anne Collins.

Finally there are the many employees that I spoke to and worked alongside without whose contribution I should have had little material to use.

preface

October 1971

First what this book is not! It is not an academic, exhaustive, over-poweringly documented or, I trust, unreadable treatise. Nor does it attempt to 'reveal all' in the field of motivation and work structuring, for the simple reason that I do not claim to know all. And it will not condemn nor elaborate upon differing hypotheses put forward in recent years by various behavioural scientists. I leave that debate to my academic colleagues.

The criterion I have applied to the cases in this book is not 'is it correct', or even in a moral sense 'is it right', but simply 'can managers use this information?' But I end each case with a question, and their answers to these will substitute for judgement.

The book will, I hope, help to bridge a gap between academia and the managers, the chasm that separates research and application, theory and practice. Little is known about the ways in which behavioural science knowledge is actually used within industry: on the one hand the scientific community often refuse to accept the dual responsibility for disseminating their knowledge to management as well as academic audiences; on the other hand those managers who have used a behavi-oural science approach have not always distributed the results of their work.

I have however followed my own interests, and this book was written in the belief that work is more efficient when it is enjoyable, that if man is not allowed to broaden his horizons he can only become obsolete. In Britain, as in so many industrial countries, there is no room for the unnecessary limitation on the maximising of our manpower, no room for the manager who is frightened of change. It seems important in this present wave of industrial unrest and economic discontent not how we change, or when we change, but that we do change. I feel there is less to fear from the reactions to explained and enlightened change than there is to fear from the reaction to *no* change. The real test for management, unions and the public generally will be in its *ability* to cope with that change.

Preface

February 1973
In presenting this new edition very little within the case studies needs alteration, for the passage of time has endorsed their validity. It is difficult for me to judge whether the problems associated with man-management and our human resources are occurring more urgently, more frequently or more publicly. Whichever the case, Government, institutions and the public generally seem to an unprecedented degree to be concerning themselves with our compelling need to become more efficient and reduce industrial conflict. Obsession with economic growth, more equal distribution of a country's income, and efficiency has resulted now in terms like decentralisation, job enrichment, organisational development, corporate planning and rationalisation becoming quite fashionable.

In the two years that have elapsed since I wrote this book, more companies have sought the practical direction of job enrichment as an answer to some of their industrial ills. Most noticeably in the last two years the country that led the research into this field, namely the USA, has lost its lead to countries such as Japan, South Africa and, more recently, the Scandinavia countries and Britain. As all societies advance they are encountering varying problems in the working environment. I have touched on some of these problems within the book and have added a case study, that of the Volvo Group, as I felt their contribution to solving some of these problems was of value to the reader.

Certainly the problems indicated in this book are taking a great deal more of management's time today than they did a few years ago and their urgency has increased rather than decreased. The greatest test is still with management, unions and the public generally in their ability to cope with these problems and tolerate and be equipped with the necessary skills for *change*.

LYNDA KING TAYLOR

SECTION ONE

chapter one

'For all we take we must pay . . . but the price is cruel high.'

Rudyard Kipling

All of us in management have an abiding concern with, for or about people. We cannot escape from the fact that we are in the people business, whether or not we be tough, autocratic, paternalistic, only-in-it-for-the-money managers. Whether we want it or not the toil of everyday work life from cleaning canteens to negotiating multi-million oil deals is undertaken by people. People are vital and the innovative firm of the future will be a people-intensive firm depending on the human resources of imagination, initiative and creativity. Fewer people may be necessary to produce a given result, but they will quickly become the necessary few without whom managers would be left sitting idle in mahogany corridors.

It will be appreciated then that if a company is to get the best out of the people who work for it, its managers had better understand what motivates people, or to put it another way, what makes people tick. New developments, operations, tasks, increased work loads cannot be effective, or improved productivity achieved, unless employees' needs, wants, aspirations, thoughts, fears and frustrations are taken into account. If we want people to give their best to their work we have to respond to their needs. There is no simple answer to 'what motivates people?' No-one has as yet produced a recipe for success in explaining and predicting human behaviour in all circumstances, or even a very wide range of circumstances. It will almost certainly never be found.

For a fuller understanding of motivation, the first step is to understand the kinds of needs man has; the second step is to create an environment and to provide incentives which will allow him to maximise the satisfaction of all those needs.

All human behaviour is determined by the wants and needs of indivi-

B   3

duals and all behaviour aims at satisfying one or more of those needs, although one is almost invariably striving for satisfaction of more than one need at a time. In view of the important relationship between needs and human behaviour, it is worth discussing the levels of need that a normal adult is subject to, and to acknowledge their existence. Figure 1 illustrates this diagrammatically.

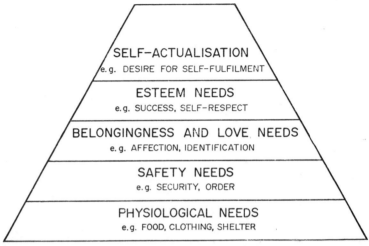

Figure 1 Maslow's hierarchy of needs.

Man is not born with a complete set of needs; at birth like any other animal he is dominated by the need to survive. Until the need to breathe, eat, rest or drink no longer requires all of his energy, the second order of needs, those of safety, assume no importance. Throughout life the physical needs of food, clothing, shelter will take precedence over all others.

The need for safety includes the present assurances that our future physical needs will be met as well as that of bodily safety. The young child continually asks 'whys and wherefores' not so much in an attempt to understand the surrounding environment but more in order to perceive a coherent structure and feel safe. Later on in adult life, the 'whys and wherefores' are intrinsic to his need to know . . . people have a deep curiosity and like the importance of being 'in on the thing'. They need to know also that there is security of income and employment in order to have the means to the end in satisfying the dominant material needs.

Feeling secure, the third and again higher level of need, that of love and belonging, will begin to preoccupy man. People need a sense of belonging to a worthy group, at first within school, later teams and organisations, societies and clubs, and perhaps ultimately the membership of a church, trade union, political party, or indeed a company, will help to meet this need. The need to share the values and attitudes of other people and to have relationships with other individuals must be satisfied before the ego needs of esteem and self-respect can emerge and increase the appetite for success and 'well done'. It is in realising this ego need that an individual will pursue his own interests in life, determine his own attitudes and values even to the risk of ostracism.

Survival assured, the jigsaw of the world no longer so much of a puzzle, friendships and love found, conscious of his own worth and the respect of others, man is then free to explore the most mature need of all, that of self-actualisation. It is this need of desire for self-fulfilment, dignity, the ability to be able to contribute to life that is so all embracing that it may take up the bulk of a working life without ever being fully satisfied.

The normal adult is subject to all five levels of need; he cannot leave three outside the factory gate and take two inside to work with him. He goes in to work with them all and will attempt to satisfy them all either at work or through work. How do the needs operate therefore in an industrial setting?

In a modern industrial state most workers earn sufficient wages to look after their basic material comforts outside of work; very few of us beg for food. In addition to this, companies provide pleasant working surroundings from duck-egg blue cafeterias to imported *Juniperus Communis* of a similar colouring for various typing pools. With optimum conditions in heating, lighting, hours of work, not to mention air flow, relative humidity or temperatures under x, y and z of given conditions, it may be accepted that physical working conditions are on the whole comfortable within the US. They are an essential factor in alleviating dissatisfaction: certainly bad conditions can have an adverse effect on health and happiness. However, an improved working environment once supplied to the work force will soon be forgotten; although it may make good morale better, it certainly will not create it.

As I mentioned earlier, in order to satisfy our dominant material needs we must have security of income. Pay is therefore a powerful need, but is one of the least powerful incentives except under certain conditions, for instance during periods of inflation or when generally wages are low. Unfortunately, people have been taught that money is the key to satisfaction, so if they feel that something is unfair at work or amiss with their lives, they will naturally ask for more money. It is not unrealistic to think that if all we give man for his work is money then he is going to do all that is possible to get as much as he can. Consider the frequent waves of wage demands in the UK. Although some are credible and realistic demands for more money, others stem from sources where conditions are unsatisfactory and workers feel that they deserve extra £'s as an incentive to offset the disadvantages of their working environment. The demands certainly indicate that the workers want something, unfortunately the demand doesn't necessarily tell us what.

It never ceases to amaze me the number of managers I encounter who rehearse the features of the good old days, and clearly have not accepted the fact that what satisfied our fathers 20 years ago does not satisfy the sons of today . . . and that this is how it should be.

Those people who are very badly off and oppressed usually accept their state of living. The discontent occurs when the goals of the ideal state of living are almost within grasp. As long as high pressure advertising depicts colour television as being a necessity of life, and as long as HP terms whet the appetite for deep freezers and miscellaneous gadgets, bringing them within reach of all, the demands for more and more pay will be heard in an attempt to bridge the gap between what people want and what they actually have or can reasonably expect to have. Therefore, pay must be such as to obtain what are considered the comforts of life. Pay must be fair in terms of the contribution being made and realistic in comparison with what other people in the company are making, as well as for similar work undertaken in a company down the road.

Material security is only part of the make-up of our 'safety' need. The security of information is another vital factor. The child's 'whys and wherefores' develop in the adult world into the wide field of communication. This field within industry alone has been the sole subject of many books and therefore I do not propose to delve and discuss the technicalities here. House magazines, training sessions, briefing groups, attitude surveys, morale researching, suggestions schemes, company participation outings, etc., etc. coupled with the more sophisticated forms of chit-chat, sensitivity training for example, take similar forms to physical working conditions. They may be necessary to avoid discontent, but certainly will not motivate employees to do a better job; however, I will agree that in many instances they will stop them from doing a bad one. Communication, therefore, like pay is essential; the same is true of training. Motivation cannot cure technical or clerical incompetence. People must know their present job, they must be allowed to use all their skills and knowledge which contribute to that work, for security is shaken if they cannot do the job well or indeed if they do not realise they are doing the job well. True security is reaped from knowing how valuable one is within an organisation.

Training for future growth is as important as training for the present job. Security need is threatened when automation or equally sophisticated systems are being considered and the employees, aware of this perhaps via a grapevine or through an official channel of communication, are not allowed to meet this change by increasing and/or changing their skills. Even if on-the-job training is no longer applicable, training in the human relation skills, better forward planning, efficiency, etc. will continue indefinitely.

Knowing the health of the company, knowing where their job fits into the organisation and knowing they will not be laid off are all essential factors to be considered in the 'security or safety' need. I have encountered many employees who have ignored financial incentives through fear that the rate for the job was going to be cut or even that they may work themselves out of a job. Hence it is useless selling craftsmen the ideals and excellences of a productivity deal in terms of satisfying their opportunity for challenge and advancement when it carries with it the threat of redundancy. Until management offers security of the job the craftsmen will be deaf to the proposals of achievement. Obvious as this may be, how many times have managements argued the concept of this kind of deal with the unions, an unkind dispute, especially when the two sides are disagreeing on two entirely different levels of need in the human being. The frequency of this kind of dispute is evidence that union negotiators as well as management must share equal opportunities in human relations training, if they are to discuss at an equitable level.

An article appeared in the *New Statesman and Nation* in 1948 which I think is worthy of repetition today. It was written by Pearl Jephcott who worked as a factory hand in a UK factory:

'Hours and pay were good, and the surroundings light, airy and gaily painted. We have all the standard facilities, a first-rate canteen; nurses; hot water; music while you work; pension schemes. We see notices about cricket and tennis, but the only voluntary activity which has touched my mate or me was the Derby Sweep. Here are my mate and I, grown women, and with the firm for three months, and we know less of the how and why than any visitor who gapes round of an afternoon. We know nothing of its history, war record, personalities, triumphs—the human story, which to quote our magazines, would touch our little womanly hearts. Profits, losses, experiments, difficulties—where the raw materials come from, where our two thousand boxes each day go off to—who knows? And, of course, we know nothing whatever of our firm's part in the production drive. Are we hitting the target? Have we got a target?'

Miss Jephcott continued:

'We shouldn't care if we did know? My hunch is that such an assumption underestimates our goodwill and our wits. If that's how management assesses us, I'd say it's too witless itself to realise what social and economic reforms, plus a couple of wars, have done to raise the level of the traditional female factory hand. I've another hunch, that we women are incurably altruistic. We've a passion to be useful—to a person. And some of us would extend this feminine vice from our private life to our job if we only realised that anyone's well-being depended on us in the national economic crisis or even in this unintelligible concern.'

That was over 20 years ago. Has it far changed to this day? I encounter many factories with the most perfect working conditions as in Miss Jephcott's day but oh! what living conditions.

In the next chapter I shall discuss man's more mature needs within an industrial context which are daily being recognised by managers as the paraphernalia of 'welfare' gets more costly. Carrot incentives are no longer rewards but a right. They have become unreasonable as managers start to rack their brains in the hope of finding new carrots either to attract an employee to join a company as opposed to another down the road, or to make an employee stay with a company. I agree that the free medical facilities, pension schemes, sickness benefits, 35 hour week may make employees join a company but they will not stay unless the firm realises their needs as human beings; and that 'the price is cruel high' when people become merely components in a company production system.

chapter two

'He smote the rock of the national resources, and abundant streams of revenue gushed forth.'

> Daniel Webster, drawing an analogy
> from Moses

Recently, one in four of the male undergraduates at Cambridge were asked to complete a questionnaire the purpose of which was to survey some of the reasons why UK industry is not able to recruit its full share of the available graduate talent. The purpose of the survey was to determine the undergraduates' attitudes towards industry. The entire report is worth reading (*Attitudes towards Industry*. British Institute of Management 1970) but the main conclusion of the survey was that out of 871 replies to the section on the features *thought* to be absent from industry (thus making it an unattractive career) 97 per cent considered that industry lacked sufficient opportunity to be creative and for original work, and 77 per cent of the replies doubted the sufficiency of the intellectual challenge industry could offer. Even more disturbing were some of the replies to the section on features found in industry which make it an unattractive career. A very high percentage recoiled from the danger they believe exists of becoming involved in the rat race and of losing their individual identities. Whether the students obtained their unfavourable impressions from recent graduates now working within industry or from their own vacation job experience is immaterial. Even if industry feels that these views are ill founded there must be scope for modifying these impressions if industry is to attract the high calibre of managerial expertise necessary to meet the challenges presented by this ever changing and competitive world. Unless industry creates the environment necessary for satisfying man's 'higher' psychological needs—the opportunity for challenge, achievement, identity, creativity—it cannot possibly hope to achieve the results that it would like from its employees.

The fact that the graduates considered that they would lose their

9 ✓

Not for bread alone

identity within an industrial setting is, as I say, even more disturbing than the other factors mentioned because work identification and a sense of belonging are part of man's social needs which must be met within life to stop him from being dissatisfied. How often do people meet us and after the 'who are you?' are we greeted with the 'what do you do?' It is the occupation that binds him into society, fits him into his social context... work and industry are the main sources of status. It will be noted that work is a social activity when we encounter people working when it is no longer financially necessary, and when retired people return to the work fold to participate in the social events. Often people who have left industry and part time work is offered in the busy season will return to meet their old friends and belong again in the social centre of the factory. The sense of identity, belonging to a worthy group, is not a motivator in the work context, it is a necessity. People will often form themselves into an 'informal' work group if membership of the 'formal' work group proves frustrating and does not allow them to be identified with management goals. The size of the production unit gets larger. The result; manufacturing workshops get lost within the vast corporation of automation, typists and clerks beg for an identity from the sprawling bureaucracy of open plan, and machinists aimlessly search for their place of belonging somewhere in the geometry of the organisation map. I have on one occasion asked a chargehand who his boss was and he answered 'the TUC'. After perusing the organisation chart I could hardly disagree with him, for it was impossible to see where he fitted into the production process. A sense of identity is a prerequisite for employee motivation and can be engineered initially through good communications and control of the size of the working group.

It will be seen later on in the case study section how paramount communication and understanding are in the field of motivation and job enrichment. Without a first class exchange in either of the former pair, it is doubtful whether the latter could ever prove successful. However, effective communication is not sending junior managers on courses and conferences that they learn all from running an efficient 30 minute chit-chat session to effective leadership. This not only proves expensive, but frustrating should the delegates be returning to the mortuaries of industry. Only doers of the word and not hearers only can rectify many of the inefficiencies in organisations' communications structures.

This is the generation that cannot turn back. I do not foresee corporations becoming smaller; I do not envisage the death of automation, but rather an acceleration of the technological pace, or a decrease in the effect computerisation and technology can have on the monotony and impersonalness of jobs. Therefore the sooner we learn to cope with the management-of-the-size problem, and discover how to manage it from the human wellbeing point of view, the better. (F/N)

Although I promised in my preface a book which was not academic or oppressively documented I hope I shall be forgiven for explaining in further detail the question of group identity before progressing to the meeting of man's most mature needs within an industrial setting.

A fundamental distinction in social psychology is that of the 'primary' and 'secondary' group. Typical examples of the primary group are the family, play groups, the neighbourhood group and also the 'natural' work group, that is the face-to-face group of between eight and twelve who make up for instance a football team. More than this number normally allows the group to subdivide. Therefore, the size of the working group is important, for its face-to-face value loses communication impact if the number is allowed to increase.

In the 'primary' group, the members are related by a network of personal relationships and no matter what these relationships are made of, each member of the group has pretty clearly defined attitudes towards each other member in that group, and the group is characterised by this face-to-face contact and cooperation. The larger bodies in which these natural units function are described as 'secondary' groups, and these are altogether more formal. The attitudes of the individuals of the 'primary' group towards the 'secondary' group are determined by the degree of visible identification, that is to say how the goals of the 'secondary' group coincide with those of the 'primary' group individuals.

Therefore, if a worker sees that the goals or interests of his own company conflict with those of his 'primary' group then no amount of pleas from head office or company propaganda will win him over, or get him to develop any sense of loyalty to his 'secondary' group. What is, perhaps, a little difficult to explain in theory can hopefully be appreciated if we view in practice the tenacity of the 'primary' group with regard to 'sympathetic' strikes.

The 'primary' group is the influence in regulating an individual's behaviour through which he acquires his opinions, goals and ideals. When no 'primary' group control occurs then the phenomenon of mob psychology arises, for when everyone is anonymous and without feeling of identity and loyalty, inhibitions are thrown aside and crowd or mob-like activities can occur. This only happens in the absence of a 'primary' group within which the size is limited, members are known, as are each person's function and each inter-personal relationship. It will be obvious from the case study section how important the size of the working group is, especially on assembly line work.

This need to be a member of a 'primary' group is, as I said earlier, an accepted principle in psychology and I would like to refer the reader to the appendix bibliography if wishing to pursue the hypothesis further. The important point for the manager is that in attempting to change human behaviour his attempt must be made through the medium of the 'primary' group rather than through any particular individual within that group. Although one can only motivate individuals, one will not get very far in this attempt if little consideration is given to his work group. In the Shell UK case study it will be seen how, with understanding and training, flexibility was obtained within a shift team, but equally how flexibility was not possible across shift teams. The 'primary' group became a strong social group and did not encourage disorganisation, albeit only temporary.

The identification with a 'primary' group is essential, and its identification with the 'secondary' group necessary. In industry this should be formulated through the working group of effectively no more than 12 people, and eight would be a desired number under most circumstances. It is interesting to note that in some areas of severe industrial unrest within UK companies the size of the working group was often as high as 50 and sometimes ashamedly higher. It is not too surprising therefore, that if the opportunity is lacking for the 'primary' group need and activity, that unstructured and, in some instances, mob-like activity will take its place. This may seem like ordinary common sense and it is sad we have to resort to some psychology and theorising to justify the existence of a reasonably sized working group. One can only assume that the reason they exist in far too few of our organisations is that common sense is not so common.

I have discussed briefly work in its role of providing for our physical requirements, and also our social needs ranging from man's requirement of fellowship in one form or another to work being an essential in life as the purveyor of status and binding within society.

I have also discussed the fact that morale of the worker is not created by the material conditions of work although they are essential requirements in the avoidance of the pain of complaint and discomfort. The cluster of conditions ranging from satisfactory lighting and noise abatement to pay and pensions are part of the job context, the environment in which the job is performed. If this is not congenial it will lead to dissatisfaction and they will continually require replenishing if dissatisfaction is to be allayed continuously.

The requests and demands for increases in these material comforts will be heard as loudly and as strongly as the plea for food when hungry or oxygen when starved of air. And no matter how plentiful the supply last week, when deprived of them today, it hurts. Until they become once again obtainable, life's survival appears dependent on it.

If the factors I have mentioned in the previous pages are necessary for the allayance of job dissatisfaction, what then is considered conducive to the promotion of job satisfaction? If improvement in the job context serves to relieve us of the dissatisfied employee and of his possible rendering of 'less than a fair day's work' the obtaining of extra effort and commitment to a task in hand can only be realised by managers when they consider what people *do* as well as how they can be treated.

· The need to promote the growth of the human mind is a principle fundamental in most political and even moral systems, and within industry we have long learned to do much for man's basic needs of providing for material and social requirements but do little for 'higher' psychological needs of achievement, challenge, for self-expression and self-fulfilment. We have got away with this state of affairs for so long simply because, unlike denial of man's physical needs which produce complaint, the refusal to cater for his psychological needs does not bring the plea of 'I want more recognition'—merely an apathy, a lack of initiative and interest. And giving him more 'carrots' does not always remove the apathy, laziness and disinterest. And no matter how big the carrot this week, by next week one will be hungry again.

In many instances, man's needs have been ignored for so long that he has stopped growing psychologically. When man no longer experiences this kind of development, he starts to die. Is it any wonder then that we experience low efficiency, certified (and uncertified) absenteeism, disinterest, resentment, bloody-mindedness and go-slows when we are managing dying people desperately wanting survival? These traits certainly indicate that man wants something, but do not necessarily indicate *what*.

Managers in a number of ways attempt to change this state of affairs. Perhaps the most common is giving a bigger 'carrot', but if that proves too costly then they apply their own brand of psychology. That is to induce the discontented to produce more by, for example, distributing a circular letter from the mahogany corridor telling their workers how their inefficiency is disrupting the economy, the company and the balance of payments. Trying to change matters by offering a friendly tête-à-tête and public lecturing is a sheer waste of time and effort once friction and tensions have developed. Adding to the Everest of paperwork without actually *doing* anything has the same effect as sending missives to all the smokers in the UK listing the evil effects produced by excessive smoking. The least we could hope for from such a missive would be a total disregard of that message and the most would be abstinence for probably a fortnight. Only when the causes for the apathy, laziness, disinterest have been removed can we expect to enjoy an improvement. Attempts at prohibition in the United States were a credible example of this. Propaganda did not remove the social or moral reasons for excessive drinking and therefore interdiction failed, even more so as no alternative to alcohol was offered to the prohibited consumers.

As I said, the state of denial in providing within industry satisfaction of man's psychological needs has been around a long time, in some instances since the turn of the century. The economic cost in restraint of opportunity for growth, advancement and creativity, in the restriction on enthusiasm, initiative and commitment is expensive and getting more so.

Britain loses over 300 million working days a year through certified sickness absence alone at an estimated cost of £1000 million a year to industry. The value in lost production was calculated for 1967–68 at £1750 million, some 5 per cent of National Income. (Rice, D. P. and Cooper, B. S. 1967 *American Journal of Public Health* 57, 1964–66, and also Office of Health Economics pamphlet *Off Sick* January 1971, page 11.)

Table 1 Comparison between 1954–5 and 1967–8 in terms of spells of sickness commencing and total days of incapacity, standardised with equivalent 1951 population. Selected causes where a trend was present.

Rises 1954–5 to 1967–8	Days %		Spells %	
	Males	*Females*	*Males*	*Females*
Sprains and strains	+267	+131	+228	+139
Nervousness, debility and headache	+189	+122	+139	+62
Psychoneuroses and psychoses	+152	+302	+68	+47
Displacement of intervertebral disc	+147	+113	+171	+132
All injuries and accidents	+72	+46	+109	+75
Degenerative and arteriosclerotic heart disease	+48	−3	+56	+23
Vascular lesions	+39	+45	+23	+10
Bronchitis	+38	+22	+19	+13
Complications of pregnancy				
Abortions				
Falls 1954–5 to 1967–8				
Anaemias	−12	−33	+2	−21
Asthma	−24	−18	−6	+6
Skin diseases	−24	−31	−30	−33
Ulcers of duodenum	−28	−32	−6	−19
Ulcers of stomach	−29	−25	−20	−23
Appendicitis	−32	−47	−41	−38
Rheumatism	−39	−55	−44	+1
Pleurisy	−44	−56	−36	−31
Respiratory tuberculosis	−83	−83	−74	−79

Source Derived from statistical information from the Department of Health and Social Security.

Certified sickness absence is the major cause of lost working time, but it is only one part of the spectrum of lost time which also includes certified industrial injury absence, uncertified sickness absence, absence without sickness and lateness. About one third of all absences lasting a short duration significantly commence on a Monday. We have all encountered the employee who ironically runs up the maximum sickness benefit entitlement within one year . . . the clerical sections of the Civil Service must share that problem. The chart at Table 1 shows that days lost for 'nervousness, debility and headache' rose by 189 per cent for males and 122 per cent for females between 1954–55 and 1967–68. Days lost from 'sprains' and 'strains' increased by 267 per cent for males and 131 per cent for females in the same period. This pattern suggests that at least part of the increase in absence rates is due to less serious illnesses being regarded as justification for absence from work. The Office of Health Economics *Off Sick* report of January 1971 stated: 'Perhaps the most significant factor associated with sickness absence, and the one which is likely to be the most susceptible to control, is the factor of job satisfaction.' The report continues:

'One of the keys to the minimisation of sickness absence, particularly short term absence, is in the hands of management. Despite the expansion of educational opportunities dull and repetitive jobs remain. It is necessary for management, through good communication and through imaginative organisation of labour, to create and maintain the motivation and satisfaction necessary to keep employees at work.'

A general revolt against this 'dull and repetitive' dissatisfying work is confirmed by perusing the Department of Employment and Productivity's earnings survey for September 1969. Foreman absences within factories were about 4 per cent compared with the semi-skilled assemblers with approximately 25 per cent. Yet it is the workers in factories who can lose pay through absenteeism, and two thirds of the reasons for lost pay were accounted for by *uncertified* sickness, late arrival, early finish or voluntary absence. F/N

Lord Robens complained that while he was Chairman of the National Coal Board he had pits where on a Monday 37 per cent of the boys were away: 'If you have 37 per cent away the pit is virtually at a standstill'. In 1970, absenteeism in the coal industry alone rose by 1.5 per cent over the previous year to 19.76 per cent. Couple with this figure that of unofficial strikes in that industry which cost the coal mining industry 3.3 million tons of production worth £21m. At one stage *voluntary* absenteeism in this industry had reached 5.77 per cent of the industry's available manpower, equivalent to a permanent labour force of 27,000 men or an annual £46 million of output. It is no wonder that Lord

15

Robens and his board considered that absenteeism and unofficial stoppages were more responsible for high cost inflation in coal and other sectors of industry than high wage claims.

Labour turnover is another costly headache. The cost of replacing a semi-skilled worker in the rubber industry alone has been estimated as at least £70 a time. With an average labour turnover figure being given in manufacturing industries at 30 per cent, a firm with 1000 employees could say goodbye to over £20,000 a year. I would hate to have the headache borne by some of the bosses in London's West End offices. Labour turnover there has been rated in the region of 65 per cent with the cost per leaver variously estimated from £60 to over £350 for a £12 to £15 per week clerk. Some turnover must be expected, but the steadily climbing rates of "voluntary" resignation coupled with the exit interview statements of 'Frankly, I didn't like the work' or 'I really didn't have a *job* to do' (and often being voiced from employees that we would like to hold on to) is certainly a matter concerning many managers. Two of the clerical and secretarial studies in the book were born from the concern of high labour turnover in these fields.

Another expense is that concerned with the double-jobbers. For financial or personal reasons, there are a large number of 'concealed' double jobbers. The Inland Revenue puts the figure at 5 million and in some parts of the UK 30 to 50 per cent of the labour force have two jobs. Naturally, there are the financial reasons for having two jobs: the trainee accountant during the the day may work in the pub at night or a newly married fireman may work his off-duty as a mini-cab driver to raise necessary cash for a new house. However, there are many people that I have met in an income bracket of over £40 per week doing another job. Many of them state that with the shorter working week they do not know what to do with their leisure and feeling fed up with TV, dogs and bingo they may as well work and be paid for it as waste their time. The problem of leisure must be one that will accompany us into the seventies. Equally, many of the double-jobbers state that they undertake secondary employment in order to relieve the monotony or frustration attributed to the primary job. A production line man in a car factory may be heard playing a trumpet in the evening and states that he enjoys being the attraction and playing solo. He enjoys being someone, which is something his primary job denies him—an actor in his day time role being denied the opportunity of playing Hamlet.

I'm not in this book going to offer comment on the fors and againsts of two jobs. However, the effect that the disease of primary job dissatisfaction bears on industry is a costly malignancy. As the secondary job is the one of choice, the priority is given to that rather than the primary one. Working in a mini-cab, band or cafe until 3 a.m. can result in the employee coming into his primary job late, which apart from adding to the bad timekeeping statistics can disrupt production line work. Similarly, the employee being so tired may choose not to come to work at all, to ensure that he is fit enough that evening for his job of choice. If the employee does decide to come into work suffering from fatigue it does not encourage efficiency, and certainly can aid accident proneness and faulty work. Table 1 showing sickness incapacity indicates that injuries and accidents at work are on the rise and according to the 1971 NIIP study are costing this country £500 millions a year.

Over a period of time the physical and mental strain of double-jobbing can be dramatic according to age and the type of secondary job. However, fatigue and subsequent insomnia carry other brands of ailments, for instance a general lowering of resistance to minor complaints, with the common cold becoming a frequent symptom on an employee's extended sickness incapacity certificate. Not all double-jobbing is adverse, but the indiscriminate 'moonlighters' can have far reaching ill effects, with a costly psychological, physical and economic price tag.

As I said earlier we are the generation that cannot turn back. Having heard an eminent voice lately contend that by the middle eighties the bulk of the world's industries and business will be controlled by only 200 mammoth corporations, then the problem of maintaining any sort of individuality and identity for the human being is going to be very real indeed. Even seeking identity with the union could be difficult, for as corporations grow it is not unreasonable to suppose that unions will do likewise. I would not be too surprised to note at the beginning of 1980 that many unions have merged and that there may only be 10 unions altogether in the UK. DATA are discovering the benefits of integration with the AUEW and marriage is proposed for the TGWU and the NUVB. This brings into one union two-thirds of the motor industry's workers. A merger is also possible between the TGWU and the AUEW. Smaller unions must follow suit.

Dissatisfaction with work, and the anonymity of sprawling work groups, bad communication systems, industrial disruption, all point towards an answer to the question 'What is the best proposition?' To pose this question alone implies *change*, which few deny.

I meet managers in UK industry who agree that change is necessary—almost everyone is agreed on wanting change. They may not agree on what sort of change and almost certainly agree that it is everyone else who should change and not themselves. Industrial executives state that it is the Government at fault and it is they who should change. Government replies that unions and their structure must change, unions in their turn blame management who argue back placing the blame at the feet of competitors who maintain that the rest of industry must change if things are to get any better. Seldom will a company admit that whole-sale, far reaching changes are necessary within its own walls.

17

I have also met many managements with good intentions who call in consultants and other types of company doctor for the purpose of diagnosing and curing undesirable situations, such as high labour turnover or low productivity. Many never follow through the St James epistle of 'Be ye doers of the word and not hearers only', in many instances because they are not prepared to accept the fact that management themselves have to share a large part of the blame for bringing the adverse situation about. In an even higher number of instances nothing is done for the reason that the company doctors, work study advisors or behavioural scientists can seldom offer an easy, quick, cheap and dramatic solution to the problems encountered.

How can it be easy, quick and cheap when the problems have existed for so many years? It is foolish to expect sudden improvements and very wise to expect that for a time anyway, following any large scale changes, things may be even worse than before. It will be seen from reading the case studies on job enrichment that the deliberate attempt to build into an employee's life a greater scope for personal achievement and recognition, consciously involving him more in his task and offering opportunity for advancement and identity, demanded effort and sustained effort. All of the large scale changes depicted in the case studies concerned a large number of employees, their welfare and the jobs they were doing. Support and involvement from management at the highest level was not only essential; it was apparent.

I often hear the complaint that we cannot expect these changes to occur as long as our industry is run by 'old' middle class conservatives. That what we need are more of the American type of decision making, dynamical entrepreneurs, preferably with business degrees and holding the company reins in their hands before they reach thirty. When I pursue the issue of 'how old is old', the answers vary from 40 years and over! I personally know many old people in their twenties and early thirties, while many of the managers I met in relation to my case studies were very young and informed managers in their forties and fifties. Old age is no crime, nor is sticking to the familiar. What is dangerous is leaving the power in the hands of people familiar with situations that no longer exist and for whom our up-to-date extensions of knowledge have not arrived. Most of the case study managers would admit to having been concerned about change, and all would confirm that it was inevitable, and it appeared only common sense to do so.

Some aim to solve the problems of the human side of the organisation from the ivory towers of academia. The Owen Report accuses the Business Schools and their graduates of being 'arrogant and remote from reality and the standard of courses too low and too academic in content'. Borne into the market are 500 pages of unreadable treatise for line managers on effective communication and as many pages are taken to prove that *x* wage payment system is better for the engineering industry than *y*, with a statistic a page why this should be so. This kind of documentation has its role to play—it's best in convincing one's academic contemporaries how complete an academic one is—especially at research. In the Richard Baxendale study it will be noted that the instigation from the Board that all managers become aware of modern management theory proved an impossible request. Not only did many of the managers not have time to read the 500 pages on academic management but many shared an inability to comprehend some of the convincingly documented hypothesis. The burden was placed on the Managing Director to read all the academic works and extract the salient points for his audience of managers and union personnel. The process of change for that company (and many others) commenced with the chore and effort of reading. It is a credit to them that the chore was completed, for it is easy to appreciate why many managements take cold feet at this early stage. It is with this in mind that I have not only included at the appendix heavy works on various management subjects, but also a light and at times satirical bibliography which make for enjoyable commuter reading. They also combine the asset of being easily read with the fact that they have been written by authors with a great deal of experience and wisdom.

Change is prevented as industrialists and academics argue the effectiveness of business school education and its products. Claims about the value and role of academia are counter-claimed by equally unflattering views from the graduates as mentioned at the beginning of this chapter. The dynamical entrepreneurs even if industry did want them have no intention of entering that activity. Of the 83 graduates who left London Business School in the summer of 1970, only 25 per cent wanted to go into manufacturing industry and this despite the fact that 84 per cent had previous industrial experience. While arguing these points we could be growing our own managers as many of the companies are doing in the case study section. A million managers every day have an opportunity to help their subordinates to develop their essential skills in situations far more realistic and important than management courses and seminars. The manager rarely sees himself as a 'coach' unless encouraged. Every time he discusses a problem with a junior asking the question 'What do you think?' he is unwittingly encouraging the development of both their managerial skills. This opportunity should not be wasted. This down-to-earth approach to management training could be a valuable service of the ITBs. All too often management training is not considered as a continuous and long term process, which are two *quid pro quo* realised by the case study companies. There are many occasions when an elderly Managing Director and his team of senior executives realise, with tragedy, there is no effective management cadre ready to step into their shoes. Unfortunately, the more commonly adopted solutions to that problem are merger, takeover of a rival principally in order to secure that company's management expertise or the use of headhunters—All very drastic measures which could be avoided if management tapped its vast reservoir of talent *within* the company.

After hearing the complaints that we cannot therefore expect change until the redundancy of either all managers over 40 or the reform of all those there at present (whichever is easier), one then is subjected to complaints about the unions. It is really they who are to blame for the faults in the economy and industrial strife at present and they are solely interested in pay and physical working conditions. I will agree that for the last 100 years they have been primarily concerned with a 'fair day's wage' and will continue to have that at the top of their list of priorities acknowledging their prime aim universally to protect and improve the living standards of their members. But trade unions, like managements, which have the interests of its members at heart or should have, must be perceptive and, indeed, responsive not only to changes in the work environment but also to changes in the work situation in general. It is interesting to see from the Volkswagen study that German trade unions have the same priority of wages and conditions as their UK counterparts. However, one of the other main priorities for the German union IG Metall is that 'it has to ensure the dignity of the worker has not been demeaned'. From the study, it will be seen how involvement and the work itself are the main factors in ensuring the dignity of the worker is maintained. Many union personnel in this country are aware of what is going on, and this was endorsed in a trade union viewpoint towards industry and the individual given in March 1968 by the Transport and General Workers Union. (This is printed as a discussion paper by the Marlow Association.) That union stated:

> 'Together management and trade unions, from their official standpoints, should do everything within their power to ensure that the worker not only derives an adequate income from his work, but is able to develop his talents and personality at the work place'.

Considering that that union has approximately 1,600,000 members covering about 200 industries, a decision not only to acknowledge change but to engineer it could have wide and beneficial repercussions.

The President of the TUC, John Newton, at the 1969 Trades Unions Congress also quelled any beliefs that the leadership at Congress House did not know what work meant to the worker when he hammered home with:

> '. . . Where work gives little or no satisfaction to the workers, where there is no freedom to exercise talent or skill, where men

and women do not determine how they do their work, they have, during their working lives lost their identity as individuals. Nobody who has not experienced the effects of years of confinement within the walls of mass production, without apparent means of escape, can understand the debilitating effect on the mind, the vocabulary, on the spiritual capacity of human endurance'.

Perhaps one of the factors that impressed me most about German industrial relations was the capability of the shop steward. Alienation between work forces and production processes was clearly apparent to this level of union representative, for not only was he trained to appreciate this, but he was responsible and involved in correcting the problem. There are many highly intelligent, devoted and responsible shop stewards in this country who should be given the chance to show it in any positive way. However, dramatic pieces of oratory from union leaders do not get the *practical* follow-up they deserve, lower down in the union structure.

Voluntary absence, bad timekeeping, uncertified sickness, certified sprains and strains and nervousness indicate that people go sick or turn up late because they do not like their jobs, because they are made sick by their jobs. Statutory intervention of an Industrial Relations Bill cannot solve these problems, and it is these problems which are the great disruptors, in mass production particularly. The TUC must realise that their present structure is ill fitted to cope with this modern Luddite unrest, let alone a pace of change. The present TUC structure does not enable the shop floor union representative to perform his role with the same candour as his German counterpart. Union leaders offer their sensible oratory, but union representatives are unable to actually *do* anything. Not only is this the fault of the TUC, for management in this country gives limited training to the shop stewards compared with our European neighbours. Unionism in this country is bought cheaply. Again, the Volkswagen study will reiterate that management cannot afford to be complacent and passive about the role of the shop steward. Change is necessary and must be the ally of both union and management. A reappraisal is necessary in many companies of the role of the shop steward, since work situations cannot be changed and improved upon without involving him. It is such an important role for the steward that he cannot undertake it without training. To expect him to do so, and to expect him to undertake his duties efficiently and competently, is an untrue assumption that many of the mass production plants have learned to their cost. Management cannot expect fairness from the union if the battle itself is unfair, if the shop stewards are ill equipped and all the ammunition they have is the sound of their own voice. Until this situation is corrected unions must continue to remain more than half the managements' disappointment, less than half the workers' hope.

After accusing managements and unions alike of the refusal to cope with growth and change the final array of complaints is aimed at the Government: a machine overstaffed in numbers and understaffed in know-how; the discussing and tinkering with previous Government regulations without ever changing them; the report after report which recognises that mal situations do exist and which state that drastic changes must be taken at some time in the future, normally around the year 2000. There is the talk and the committees which will endorse the viewpoint that change is necessary and which adds up to an awful lot of wasted time, and little action. Many of the reports and recommendations have a Wilson label and therefore much of the content will no doubt be regarded as unsuitable for a Tory Downing Street. The Maud report is an example of this. Surely the day of a 'party' solution must be superseded by simply the day of the 'solution'?

On one visit around a car factory having difficulty with maintaining delivery schedules, an assembly line worker did not entirely blame recently experienced labour disputes. Blame was also directed at the temper of the Chancellor of the Exchequer. If the mood of the Government machine can be felt so painfully along the production line then that machine must be overhauled to acquire the knowledge and structure for coping with the changing industrial world outside, a world familiar with EEC, 'buy British' and the balance of payments being uttered by almost every school child in the country. But the blame for the assembly lines not producing more, and for the existence of deficits in export, is more often put upon industry and the unions: the former for employing export department personnel who have never been abroad, and the latter for being unkind and slapping in domestic wage demands in times of restraint because they want to go abroad. Certainly, the accused is seldom the Government machine whose export and customs service to mention but one is in a state of *rigor mortis*, caused in part by red tape, formalities and special conditions, and in the main by a paper jungle spreading from cumbersome tariffs to the complex system of special duties and exceptions. It is caused by a creaking administrative machine making the effort of selling overseas so time consuming and exhausting that it is a wonder anyone exports at all.

The Fulton report verifies that the inefficiences of management and administration are not only within the export and customs departments of the Civil Service, but states:

> 'The Home Civil Service today is still fundamentally the product of the 19th century philosophy of the Northcote-Trevelyan Report. The problems it faces are those of the second-half of the twentieth

century. In spite of its many strengths, it is inadequate in six main respects for the most efficient discharge of the present and prospective responsibilities of Government'.

It is worth mentioning the six respects:

1 It is still too much based on the philosophy of the amateur (or 'generalist' or 'all-rounder'). This is most evident in the Administrative class, which holds the dominant position in the Civil Service.
2 The present system of classes in the Service (there are over 1400, each for the most part with its own separate pay and career structure) seriously impedes its work.
3 Scientists, engineers and members of other specialist classes are frequently given neither the full responsibilities and opportunities nor the corresponding authority they ought to have.
4 Too *few* civil servants are skilled managers.
5 There is not enough contact between the Service and the community it is there to serve.
6 Personnel management and career planning are inadequate.

'For these and other defects the central management of the Service, the Treasury, must accept its share of responsibility. We propose a simple guiding principle for the future. The Service must continuously review the tasks it is called on to perform; it should then think out what new skills and kinds of men are needed and how these men can be found, trained and deployed'.

Two of the main recommendations of the report were:

'All classes should be abolished and replaced by a single, unified grading structure covering all civil servants from top to bottom in the non-industrial part of the Service. The correct grading of each post should be determined by job evaluation'.

and

'In the interests of efficiency, the principles of accountable management should be applied to the organisation of the work of departments. This means the clear allocation of responsibility and authority to accountable units with defined objectives. Departments should establish Planning Units'.

One can only hope that all the recommendations offered by Lord Fulton and his committee are put into action. It would be sad if the two year report completed within a Labour term of office proved unsatisfactory to an incumbent Conservative party. For the report points towards a renovated Government machine which is adequate for the 'discharge of the present and prospective responsibilities of Government'. The six pinpointed inadequacies of the Home Civil Service are not peculiar to that organisation; they can be shared with many members of the community it serves. If change is considered necessary it cannot be in isolation. It must indeed be the ally of the unions, management and the Government.

It seems only common sense that if you have a person on a job that he be used, and that people are the common denominator of all progress. Yet as we learned from the undergraduate survey they are not even being attracted to industry for fear of their talents being untapped. And when we have got them there? 'Cooks Tours'? The comments of 'Thank God it's Friday!' How many times have we heard the mutter as the end-of-day hooter sounds 'That's the one I've been waiting for since 7.30 this morning!' or even, God forbid, when the 7.30 a.m. hooter sounds, the retorts of 'Wished that was the second one!'

Or perhaps there are no loud comments, just the bad timekeeping, the voluntary absences, the uncertified Monday away from the office, the industrial disruption, the export figures. Can we afford the psychological debasement such as that described by John Newton and Pearl Jephcott? Can we pay the economic price as that indicated by working days lost statistics and balance of payments figures? Can we survive the 'here and now', 'all that matters is the present', 'good or bad we must make the best of it' philosophies that accompany the acceptance of disrupted assembly lines because of absenteeism, delayed delivery dates because of bad communication and the continual handshake at £70 a time to that semi-skilled worker who got fed up and tried somewhere else?

No one would disagree that efficiency is the basis of our survival. However, in its pursuit we have created a dehumanisation which we now find has created its own product of inefficiency. This situation can only be reversed by capitalising on our manpower. This will mean a long haul, long in the sense that its effects may not be felt in many instances until the next generation. It will mean risk taking and decision making, two chores which many British managers are not very professional at. The best place for those not wishing to consider or accept change and its basic ingredient of commitment is in retirement. For we have no alternative; motivation of our work force is a cure for some of our economic and industrial ills. How this has been realised by some companies is the subject of Section Two of this book.

SECTION TWO

introduction

*'I pass with relief from the tossing sea of Cause and Theory
to the firm ground of Result and Fact.'*

Sir Winston Spencer Churchill

In Section One of this book I have discussed the generalisations of
motivation, for example recognition, responsibility and achievement.
How a number of companies have translated these into the specifics
relating to everyday work is the subject of this section of the book.

Now, hopefully, we share a fuller understanding of the kinds of needs
a person has and accept the fact that he aims to satisfy these needs while
at work as well as 'off-the-job'. The questions arise: 'How do we create
an environment in which these needs can be satisfied?' and 'What
incentives can we offer that will incite an employee to want to do better?'

A better way of answering these points is by stating what other
companies have done and what for them has worked. None of the
companies will admit to having discovered the one and only best
approach in getting the best out of people, nor do they believe what they
have done within their own concerns required some special kind of
magic. It did demand concerted effort in the fields of training and communication, involvement and understanding. For as I mentioned
earlier these are necessary prerequisites for motivation. Success involved
commitment, enthusiasm, risk taking, decision making and the 'concern'
for change. Often, in my discussions with the managers involved with
the studies, the 'concern' was in the field of the future manpower that
would be available to industry. By 1973 there will be almost 800,000
school leavers in the UK who have reached the age of 18. Ten years
later this figure will have increased by 25 per cent. With the present
growth in higher and technical education, the development of universities and business schools, the calibre of the manpower attracted will be
high. In fact students in universities and other forms of higher education
will have quadrupled by the year 2000 and those in further education

will have grown at an even faster pace. The pattern of jobs must change in order to accommodate the needs of this new age of employee. Jobs must fit the abilities and aspirations of the people doing them. We are in effect entering another 'craft' era which will be related to intellectual dexterity as opposed to the traditional manual skill. Management must begin now to take some measure of this problem.

Added to this, the equal pay date in 1975 and the teaching already in progress to our young female school leavers is that factory and office jobs are no longer for two years but that they go on long after marriage. Are these girls, the technical workers and the high calibre students going to be content with automation jobs? The division of labour has escalated into the division of man, for we have assumed that although man is capable of making a nail he is not capable of also making the head of that nail. Will our future manpower accept this exploitation even if employed as wage slaves. Already the most militant and aggressive sections of the unions are the better paid ones, and the car factories have long discovered that their employee's £40 and more a week in no way tempts that worker to love his boss and his company. Will our 800,000 school leavers be any different?

At the 1970 Institute of Personnel Management's National Conference it was said that the new generation of manual workers would contain 5 per cent who would be in the top 16 per cent of a company's intellectual talent. This kind of figure would lead me to assume then, that if our future manual manpower is going to be different it is in the region of a definite 'No' to exploitation, wage slavery, boredom money and alienation. When foremen have degrees, they will not be content with supervision as many of us are familiar with it today—verification, rubber stamping, checking, disciplining and signing. Supervision in this sense must become superfluous.

The majority of the 800,000 will also be products of the classroom revolution. No longer will they be children sitting rigidly within the boundary of one room listening to absorb knowledge from a teacher. They will be the offspring of participation, having been encouraged to learn for themselves. Cheating becomes the maximising of a neighbour's resource, and project teams transgress subject and often class and school boundaries. Instead of hearing 'Silence, do not talk with your neighbour' they will have been accustomed to group discussion and a recognition stemming from the setting of their own controls with a freedom from supervision. They have been taught to challenge assumptions and authoritative management. Will this school leaver accept the traditional, authoritarian, 'Do not do as you think, do as you are told' philosophy, or will it appear so alien an experience that rebellion is inevitable? I am convinced that it will be as inevitable and as natural as it is for them to cry when in pain, to beg when without.

Then there have been other discussions with managers when the 'concern' turned its attention to those people who do not want their jobs enriched, and the people we cannot motivate. Every organisation has its 'unreachables', those people with no interest at all in a personal goal let alone a departmental one. Fortunately, there are only a few with whom maximum effort only gets minimum performance. In many instances, they can be left on their own; at other times it may be necessary to get rid of them or be continually bugged with a motivation problem. A similar philosophy applies to jobs. There are a few in any organisation which cannot be enriched. These jobs, the 'untouchables' offer no opportunity for growth, creativity or responsibility. An example of this could be the job of lift attendant. If one cannot put in charge of the office lift an 'unreachable', then the job should be automated out of existence. If the same amount of enthusiasm which is directed into concern for the 10 per cent of 'unreachables' and 'untouchables' could be transferred to solving the problem of the 10 per cent of the labour force either on strike, absent with or without leave, the double-jobbers and those shirking in canteens and toilets planning sabotage of the machine or the man who made it, we would not have to pay and pray as hard as we do that the remaining 90 per cent are not considering similar moves.

Then, there is the 'concern' that has arisen when a person's job has been enriched but no improvement has occurred, and when in some instances things have got worse. Understanding is of paramount importance in the success of any job enrichment scheme. It will be seen in the Swedish case study that the process by which a decision is reached has as much effect on the success of any resultant change as the quality of the decision. Old habits die hard and control of the job should not be camouflaged by control of the person. This was particularly relevant with some companies, methods of management by objectives and target setting. Work planning and review, target and objectives setting can be an excellent communications vehicle for transforming the individual's purpose and direction and for identifying his objective with that of the organisation. If not communicated effectively and understood properly it can deteriorate into a device for controlling people and telling them what they *must* achieve. The 'opportunity' then of management by objectives is replaced by that of 'demand' and in some instances 'surprise' (33 of them every morning I was told by one Managing Director!)

Many of the case studies indicate that when given the opportunity for personal achievement as in management by objectives, people either will achieve or they will not. At no times were things ever any worse *unless it had been wrongly communicated in the first instance* when the 'opportunity' had been wrongly interpreted as 'demand'. When this interpretation and misunderstanding occurs, the understood 'demand' can often accompany a price tag. In many of the case studies, much effort was concentrated on communication, training and understanding that in no instance did management face a demand for higher pay to match the new opportunities and responsibilities.

Insufficient training can also be a prime factor in things being worse than before, for motivation cannot cure technical or clerical incompetence. In both the clerical and secretarial studies, great emphasis is placed on ensuring that people were capable of carrying out the new and improved tasks. In all the studies it is stressed how important management support is with regard to training, and one of the fuller managerial roles is always one of ensuring that the subordinates are capable of the new job and that wherever possible an opportunity is present for the growth of latent and new skills.

Another reason why things may be worse than before centres on responsibility. Target setting must be a two way process and if a person is going to be responsible for achieving a target it must be one he has agreed to. In one company I encountered, responsibility was being sold as accountability for a higher production figure at the end of the day. Instead of producing the heads of 3000 nails, the girl was told that it would be 3500. This is certainly not responsibility and job satisfaction, but more a case of movement and efficiency. The female employee now finds that she can no longer chatter while she worked. The work cycle process has been reduced from 13 seconds to 3 and although it can be said that the girl didn't have much time to be bored, she didn't have time to be satisfied either. Apart from this it all adds to the increased figures in Table 1 for headaches and nervousness. No-one is any better off except perhaps the Organisation and Methods department. Of course, the reverse can also be true. For the same O & M department having heard that a work cycle lengthened from 3 seconds to 13 will prevent neurosis can find themselves confronted with a shop floor of very bored women. Unless the extra 10 seconds is considered worthwhile and satisfying by the individual on the job, the scheme will inevitably lead to failure.

Finally, involvement. It will be seen in all the case studies that involvement was a two way process. At no time did personnel departments go around asking people what they thought about such-and-such and then ignore their comments anyway. The 'downward consultation' provided information and advice. It is at all times considered an essential to avoid dissatisfaction, for it helps to satisfy a person's basic 'security' need for information and being in the know. It does not motivate, but forms part of the vital communication process within any firm.

What did motivate was the fuller satisfaction that came with the two way involvement of participation that is outlined in almost all the studies in one form or another: being more involved in their own work, contributing and being accountable for decisions directly affecting their own task, being responsible for their own work priorities and being self-supervisory. In fact, subordinates were now doing what was originally undertaken by their superiors, and in most instances doing it as effectively and as competently. It was this, the direct involvement and responsibility with the job itself, that motivated the subordinate.

There was 'upward consultation', but instead of it being in the form of requiring verification, for example, it was in the seeking of technical information. Instead of approaching their supervisor, in the Electricity Board study, for rubber stamping and approval, cleaners now approached him questioning a stock control and budgetary position. In this kind of communication structure there is a genuine two way motivation. For the superior is motivated as well as the subordinate. He is approached on a technical and complex commercial point, as opposed

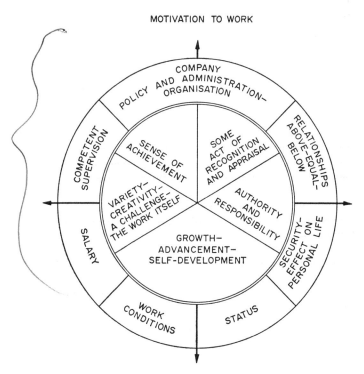

Figure 2 An illustration of what motivates individuals to work. The inner circle is job content and the motivators while the outer circle is the job context, the environment in which it is done.

31

to the original mere clerical and time consuming chore of verification and approval. He also carries the responsibility for ensuring that that same subordinate is competent to cope adequately with the challenge of self-supervision and budget accountability.

The facts in these studies speak for themselves. What perhaps is the most important 'fact' of all is that all these companies have actually 'done' something and not just attended conferences and read books on motivation. They have all attempted to follow through the epistle 'Be ye doers of the word and not hearers only' and in doing so have made some mistakes. But these mistakes have been positive ones in that they always learned from them and from the experience prevented errors occurring in the future.

It is hoped that mistakes will be even less likely in companies proposing future changes similar to those outlined in the following pages. It is with this hope in mind that the firms contributing to this book have allowed their experience to be shared.

It transpires from these studies that the situations which people find most satisfying and rewarding are invariably those which provide the opportunities that I have indicated in the *inner* circle on Figure 2. If any of the factors indicated in the *outer* circle are allowed to deteriorate in any way, as mentioned earlier, a climate of dissatisfaction and tension, frustration and friction will prevail in which people will not give of their best. Assuming, in principle, potential use for the manager of some of the concepts indicated in these studies, understanding, familiarity and practice in applying them in action are the only ways of discovering where and when they can be useful.

case study one

Richard Baxendale & Sons Ltd

'The situation in a great deal of our industry, particularly on the assembly line is that there are far too many moronic jobs. In this kind of working environment the only time the workers' needs for esteem are met is when they "beat" the management and the "system" with a weak argument. This allows them, perhaps, their only opportunity to feel a sense of achievement.'

Ian C. Smith

Director and General Manager
Baxi Heating

I would like to thank both Philip Baxendale, Managing Director, and Ian Smith, Director and General Manager, of Baxi Heating, for the time they have given in helping me prepare this study. I also appreciate their kindness in allowing the material to be published, and for providing me with every facility on my visits to Preston.

LKT, March 1971

33

Baxi Heating is a private company manufacturing domestic central heating equipment. The company has about 750 employees, and is situated near Preston. Their basic operations are in foundry work, assembly and sheet metal work. There are 10–11 trade unions within the organisation ranging from the AEF to the TGWU. The company objectives start with profits aiming for a minimum return on capital employed of 20 per cent. To attain these profits their second objective is to remain leaders in the open fire market, to take x per cent of all the open fires sold in this country. The open fire market is diminishing, with less solid fuel being used, so Baxi are trying all the time to gain an increasing share of a decreasing market. Baxi also manufacture gas water central heating equipment, and here again they want to be leaders, to obtain y per cent in a rapidly expanding market. The company are aware that by the end of the seventies the UK central heating market will be declining, therefore part of their objectives is to move into other sales areas that will enable the company to continue expansion. One of the written objectives of the company is to operate Baxi on a participation basis, for two reasons. One is that they are conscious that their employees spend up to 50 per cent of their waking life at work and therefore they, as employers, should aim to make that 50 per cent as satisfying as possible. Secondly, because they feel that they can obtain better profits if the company is operated in this way, simultaneously guarding job security, expansion, etc.

Around 1960, the company was attempting to build up a management team to cope with the expansion that was taking place and expected to continue, and became involved at top level in increasing its knowledge and understanding of management in order to 'manage' all the difficulties anticipated.

Following Lenin's philosophy of 'theory without practice is futile, practice without theory sterile', Philip Baxendale, the Managing Director, insisted that all the managers within the company obtain a knowledge of management theory and see where this could be applied within the organisation. A distributed bibliography indicated the works of many modern management theorists, and it was suggested that all managers should familiarise themselves with the suggested reading. A task simple in theory proved difficult in practice. Perhaps the reason for this lies in the first sentence of the foreword to this book, when I reiterated what I hoped this book would not be. Not an academic, exhaustive, weightily documented, unreadable treatise condemning or elaborating upon differing modern hypotheses. However Baxi found (and I am sure that they are not alone) that much of the selected management reading suffered from one or more of these ailments. Not only did some managers not have the time to consume the words of supposed wisdom, but many shared an inability to comprehend some of the more heavily documented works.

34

I would, at this point, like to mention a little of the philosophy that Baxi have used in relation to factory management. They recognise a manager as being someone who has more work to do than he can do himself, and that he must have other people to help him do his work. Once one says 'other people to help him do his work' then a manager must be responsible for the hiring and firing of those people. Many years ago Baxi decided that their foremen were managers, and as such carry the responsibility for the recruitment, selection and dismissal of their own staff. The foremen also have to ensure that their staff are equipped with the tools of the trade, to give of their best in the job, and are therefore responsible for the adequate training of their staff. The foreman has a definite manager/subordinate relationship and, naturally, quite a wide span of authority. He is considered part of the 'executive' system running the company. This 'executive' system appears as follows:

General Manager → Works Manager → Foreman → shop floor
or
Section
Manager

It is this system which is responsible for all communication downwards.

The shop steward within Baxi is someone who has been elected by his constituents to represent them in negotiations with management. He is part of the representative system of the company which does not exist to communicate to the shop floor. The shop steward is elected to negotiate. For this, he may not know the rules and therefore he too has to embark on an ambitious form of training closely related to the company and its needs in a social as well as technical system. The purpose of this training is to make the shop steward fully aware of his objectives, namely to obtain for his members security, job satisfaction and money, which it was stressed could be achieved provided that the company's profits were rising.

He takes part in exercises in learning how to negotiate and to handle situations. New shop stewards were often found to commit themselves too readily in many situations and a hard part of the learning process was the behavioural change from the promise of something that could not be realised to 'I will find out for you'. At the same time, in view of the cost of this training, agreement was obtained that a shop steward's term of office should be two years instead of one, although the union members still had the right to throw out their shop steward at any time if they considered he was not effective.

Of all management training, 80 per cent is on the job and into this training has infiltrated the Baxi belief that the greatest industrial pay-off lies in the utilisation of the full capacities of shop floor personnel and that man's psychological needs must be met to some extent on the job itself.

D

One of the written company objectives, as I said earlier, is that the company be operated on a participation basis and on the policy that, firstly, men like work and, secondly, seek responsibility and are capable of self-control. The training courses are often geared to this objective and policy and, whether for shop stewards or senior managers, are based on the need to boost productivity. And this is to be through the fuller participation that is possible with job enrichment, profit sharing schemes, work planning and review systems, and the teachings of leading management theorists. Baxi insist that they can improve task efficiency by ensuring that their shop floor men are not asked to operate like robots, that the job itself must provide the human satisfaction needs of personal achievement, challenge, responsibility and the opportunity for recognition and growth. To allow for this introduction of change, the culture and climate throughout the organisation must be right. In the company, the simple four rank hierarchy of the executive system facilitates communications. It also defines the manager–subordinate relationship clearly, adding a flexibility to the organisation structure. The climate within Baxi, after a great deal of effort and time, is considered favourable, the culture acceptable, ensuring that change can be interlinked with progress on all sides.

Perhaps one of the most valuable organs of communication within this company is its Works Council established in the early sixties. This Council consists of the General Manager and representatives from every section of the company, from the management, foremen and office level, and shop stewards representing the shop floor. The Works Council meeting is held to ensure that what is happening is communicated to everyone; it is a command meeting, with the commands generating from the General Manager. However, the commands must be understood and agreed before becoming effective. For example, if the company wanted to operate one man buses, it would seek agreement to this before buying the buses. This Works Council, meeting every six weeks, informs employees of progress, profit, sales and possible company changes, with the minutes being published for all to read.

Emphasis was placed more on work than simply the duties of a task, firstly in 1965 when the company scrapped its original and traditional form of merit review. Considered as 'non-motivating' and convinced that criticism does not motivate people, a work planning and review system was introduced, which is a simpler form of management by objectives. Each person works out his targets with his manager right down to shop floor level with standards for measuring performance being established at the same time as the targets, and both being reviewed at six monthly intervals. These individual targets are set within a framework of the company objectives.

Three examples of the work planning and review are shown, those for the Chief Buyer, Works Manager and a Factory Engineer. The targets are never imposed but are arrived at after careful discussion with the superior. The targets provide each of the individuals with an opportunity for challenge and achievement, and the responsibility for their being attained rests solely with that individual. This allows him to make his own decisions and, instead of referring back to his superior for a rubber stamp approval, he now requests technical advice and information. This is an example of the genuinely two way participation that I referred to earlier. Both subordinate and superior are motivated.

When the targets are achieved, the subordinate not only receives the feedback of result, but also the recognition from his superior. In fact, this system draws upon almost all motivators. Chance for achievement, challenging work, recognition, authority and responsibility, and the opportunity for self-initiated work, for example in the stock control improvement area which is on the target list for the Works Manager in Table 3. There is also the additional financial responsibility which can be seen in Tables 2 and 4, that is a target for the Chief Buyer to ensure a reduction in cost of components by at least 5 per cent, and in the costs of maintenance, labour and materials which are key target areas for the Factory Engineer.

Table 2 Work planning and review   *Chief buyer: Mr F. M. Newton*

Key area	Main action or opportunity	Yardstick
1 Production lines not to be stopped because of shortage or quality of Bought out materials.	Get out separate bought out cost figure.	Cost of stoppages to be £20 per week.
**2 Stock levels at minimum from financial and spare parts point of view.	Computer stock sheet improvements.	£260,00 by Feb. 1971.
***3 Price reductions without lowering quality	Make use of value engineering and training of Buyers on it. Do monthly review of price savings. Consider extending contracts. Attempt to get FMN on Buying Negotiating Course.	Target is 5% reduction on existing prices at March 1970.

Asterisks indicate priority, *** means immediate attention.

37

Table 3 Work planning and review   *Works Manager: Mr T. Hughes*

Works objectives
To produce; to Sales demand to meet altering forecast figures, as economically as possible to the required quality.

Key area	Main action or opportunity	Yardstick
**1 Improving the company productivity	Work study role becoming mainly new methods. Obtaining optimum flexibility of labour.	Obtain for each area the figure agreed at the productivity deal during the next 6 months, and shown by F. Bradley's figures.
***2 Production being ready for new product starting dates.	Set up prototype pilot assembly line. Improving performance of production development department.	Senate RC1—Sept. 70. Wooden Gas fire—Oct. 70. Direct flue—Oct. 70. Brazilia—Mid Nov. 70. Senate TT—Jan. 71. Electric Controls—Feb. 71.
**3 Production of existing products.	Production planning to have stock of Bermuda, conversions and spares.	No major shortages on Bermuda.
4 Training of Supervisors and Shop Stewards. J. Gilgun responsible to T. H.	Use of J. Gilgun.	Get more back than paid on levy.
5 Stock control improvement.		Monthly reports of C. Higginson. No large variances at stock taking.

Asterisks indicate priority. *******means immediate attention.

Table 4 Work planning and review   *Factory Engineer: Mr T. L. Sutton*

Engineering Department Objectives

(1) Maintaining machinery and services economically to enable production commitments to be met.

Key area	Main action or opportunity	Yardstick
1 *Planned Maintenance operating effectively*		
a Taccone.	Look at cycle time circuit. Make simple universal change to go from lowest cycle time to boilers.	7½ hrs per week emergency working on Taccone. Cycle time 21 or 22 sec by end of Dec. 1970.
b Rest of Factory.		All machines fully covered by planned maintenance by March 71.
2 *Costs of Maintenance Labour & Materials*	Consider a Special Current Section for production for next Budget.	As budget.
3 *Projects or Investigations*		
a Assessment of probable life of moulding boxes.		Report by end Dec. 70.
b Report on cost of filling in 'square' between Sheet Metal and Dispatch.		Report by end Dec. 70.
c Complete new Office/Reception.		By April 1971.
d Do complete electrical survey.		
e Shell moulding set up for future. Future use of new mill.	Report by I.C.S.	
4 *Productivity Schemes*		
Maintenance.		Achievement of Taccone target.
Building Maintenance.	Some reduction in labour.	Achievement of production target.

Perhaps the most difficult changes for Baxi to introduce have been with the shop floor personnel. And here, as other case studies will prove, the process of behavioural change is a slow one. A culture cannot be changed overnight. A long time ago the work study department perfected a job method and placed people in front of a machine not intending them to think. Many of them have been coming to work not thinking for years, and therefore one of the biggest problems of this decade will be the meeting of the satisfaction needs of shop floor automata. Of course, it is always easier to recognise a problem and talk about it than to apply a solution. And any changes to a familiar work pattern are often resisted.

About two and half years ago a job enrichment scheme was introduced into the gas convector assembly line. The work study team had installed a conveyor at which nine men had worked side by side. The men on this flow line were each making a part of a convector, then passing it on to the next man. This routine job, with a few minutes work cycle, was undertaken by skilled sheet metal workers. The product was inspected after manufacture by three inspectors who were also skilled sheet metal workers. The line was paid on piece work. The line had to be 'balanced', meaning that each man had to have an equal work load, while overtime requirements meant that the whole line had to be available. It was felt that a complete job would be much more satisfying than the routine job and it was decided to change the operation to each man making up a complete gas convector himself. In changing over to the new method of production the piece work pay system was to be replaced by a relatively high standard daily rate.

This is where concerted effort at ensuring an efficient training and communications network within Baxi proved most valuable. The executive and representative systems plus the Works Council had all been subjected to the vigorous training schedules indicated earlier. On-the-job courses included also the shop stewards watching the Gellerman management film series which depicts the theories of motivation and, practically, describes their potential and application. ['Motivation and Productivity' film series (BNA films).] It was considered that the idea had been 'sold' and put across to the men. It was therefore agreed that the production line men should be provided with the correct training to enable them to manufacture an entire gas convector and not merely a component.

As I said, the line had been on piece work and as such was one of the best paid lines in the company. The company made two mistakes at that time. One was that they viewed job enrichment as an end in itself, and the realisation that it is caught up with the wages attitudes and cultural framework of a company was not fully appreciated until after the second mistake. This was that Baxi, in concentrating on man's higher need for the responsibility and satisfaction of doing a complete job, overlooked the basic need of pay.

As I said earlier in the book, pay must be fair in terms of the contribution being made and realistic in comparison with what other people in the company are making. To replace the piece work system by a standard daily rate meant that the *new* rate had to be at least the same as a *piecework* pay packet. This, of course, meant that the new daily rate would be much higher than for comparable jobs within the company. To go ahead with this scheme would have meant that skilled craftsmen, maintenance, pattern shop employees, etc. would all slap in a pay claim to management in order to be brought into line with the new daily rate on assembly. Management could not afford this mass of claim and therefore the semi-skilled assembly men were to earn *less* on the new wage system than on the old piece work. The assembly men believed that part of the job enrichment exercise was to bring them into line with the rest of the company. Agreed prices could not be arrived at and assembly demanded to stay on piece work.

Of course, the assembly men would not accept the state of affairs that management proposed. Trying to satisfy man's achievement need while simultaneously cutting the rate for the job is a proposal any shop floor would be deaf to . . . and at Baxi they were. They were blind to the responsibility and satisfaction because their basic security was threatened. However, this abortive trial was not considered to be anywhere near a failure. For the men certainly found the job more satisfying, and being responsible for their own finished product the quality of that product improved by about 200 per cent. An absenteeism rate of 6 per cent on that line dropped to 1 per cent. Each of the men certainly enjoyed being given the opportunity to develop his own competence and, coupled with the self-supervision resulting in the improved quality of product, it was considered that these reasons alone were enough to convince Baxi that the mistake with the wages system must be turned to good account. They must learn from it and prevent it from happening in the future.

Since that time, two and half years ago, Baxi have made several attempts at the elimination of piece work. They have succeeded on some jobs but there have been difficulties. One attempt was made by management at the wrong time, for there was a dispute on and no-one would consider differentials when a basic wage claim was on the desk of the Managing Director. 'A clever management way of trying to dock the claim' was the shop floor attitude to management's trying to eliminate piece work and consider differentials when the basic rate was at fault. First things first and that means security. Thus the dispute was settled and Baxi immediately set up an advisory panel to look at productivity and differentials. The three man team consisted of the Work Study

Manager, the Convenor of shop stewards and a shop steward from the sheet metal department. This team visited a number of well known companies which had productivity deals, and discovered for themselves that in most of those companies the management and shop floor views of particular aspects of the productivity bargain differed considerably.

When the team returned it was decided to agree differentials, even if they could not be brought into effect right away. This was accomplished within three weeks using the direct consensus method of job evaluation. To put this simply it is the comparing of one job against another. A differential table with eight groups was produced. Then, for working out the productivity deal, each group was taken on its merit and told that they must turn out a measure for each area that would affect the company profitability. The Management Accountant was brought in to talk to the groups who said that, if the company was going to make a profit out of the operation of that department, then a scale of payback would depend on effort of work, method of work and the differentials.

This would be agreed separately for each area, and each area would form its own productivity committee. The objective of that committee is achieving greater productivity and therefore greater earnings for the men. No money is given out to any group in the company without their having earned it in productivity. The shop floor, through their productivity committee, approach their management with ideas for changing working methods to improve the productivity situation within the respective groups. Productivity is being tackled on a realistic basis for each area, and the people within that area carry personal responsibility for the production which achieves company profitability. It is participation with an objective; to get more money, more job security and to stay in business. With a training curriculum informing the executive and representative systems how to get the best out of people, foremen and shop stewards alike realise that one gets far more out of a person if they are interested in their work and if they feel committed to their task. Individuals develop an enthusiasm and *want* to give more and do more, if they are satisfied with the job as well as the pay. Now, within the framework of the productivity pay package, job enrichment on the gas convector assembly has been successfully introduced. The assemblers are no longer the components in a production process.

The opportunity for more challenging and responsible work, with the added dimension for skill growth and promotion within the grades, now promotes ideas and cooperation from the shop floor. In one year there has been a 10 per cent increase in productivity in the foundry. There is no taking advantage of this on the part of management. They realise that more is being achieved, and that the shop floor is being more competent and, carrying the authority for their own work, are also taking on more responsibility.

For this the workers in the foundry have received an 8 per cent increase in their wages. This is coupled with the satisfaction of a more interesting and exacting job on individual assembly, of being involved in a complete task and not merely acting as a robot.

Management at the same time are realising the benefits through easier alteration to outputs and overtime working as the lines are no longer 'balanced' with individual assembly. There is also a greater flexibility of labour and a higher quality of product.

The foreman has time to be a manager instead of exerting the discipline considered necessary on a flow belt system. As other studies in this book will endorse, the foreman has more time to devote to his staff and technical development, not having to be always 'on the job'. He has more time to consider the training his subordinates will require in extending their skills to cope with having a 'complete' job. He is able to attend training for his own development of management responsibility. After all, no-one tries to be a physicist without studying physics, so why should people try to be managers without studying management. They are both professions. Making management professional almost seems to be a company objective within Baxi.

Within this company job enrichment and participation have gone hand in hand, complementary to one another. Perhaps the authenticity of this was realised a few months ago when the subordinates made the initial move in approaching their management on a matter for which they carried a personal responsibility. The two shifts of a foundry, their productivity committees and shop stewards requested to meet in their own time, on a Saturday morning. They wanted to discuss the productivity deal and responsibility for their particular area, and to discuss the job content and methods for achieving respective objectives. They requested a long question and answer session, for they needed understanding and the knowledge that management were 'with' them, giving them capable support.

Baxi are quick to admit that job enrichment is no simple panacea. This is one way to get the best results. The returns on management development are intangible since there can never be any finished product. Getting the best out of people is a continuous objective, just as constant as a minimum return on capital.

The company has aimed at satisfying the needs in their entirety for its individuals, through the task those people are engaged on. They have aimed to make the tasks themselves motivational; to have and to offer a purpose. It was this that two shifts discussed of their own choice, in their own time, with their management on that Saturday morning. Can effective self-development have a better criterion?

case study two

Dexion-Comino International Ltd

It is not always the most efficient arrangement to break a job down to the simplest elements. The results can be utterly monotonous and boring, with little real concern from the person involved in meeting the company objectives.'

Geoffrey Gilbert

Head of Personnel Services
Dexion-Comino International Limited

I am grateful to Demetrius Comino OBE, Chairman, and Geoffrey Gilbert, Head of Personnel Services, of Dexion-Comino International Limited, for providing me with many details relating to this study and for allowing it to be published. I would also like to thank Susan Holmes King, the company's Commercial Training Officer, for giving much time and effort in discussing the study with me.

LKT, March 1971

In 1947 Demetrius Comino launched Dexion Slotted Angle, a new idea in construction that was not only to grow into a new industry but to grow, within 23 years, into an international organisation with a turnover in 1970 of £30m.

The story is a source of inspiration to all small companies who are prepared to think along progressive lines not only about production, but about management. Demetrius Comino started his own company in the late twenties within the printing trade. Coming into the business young, and with a fresh mind free from preconceptions, he made a significant contribution to printing production.

Printing is however not so much a product as a service and Mr Comino wanted a product that could be made in volume and would fulfil his creative urge. A clue to an unsatisfied industrial need already existed within his own company; the problem of space. As the business grew it was necessary not merely to add to existing facilities but to arrange and rearrange plant for greater and more efficient output, involving constant dismantling and rebuilding of equipment. The usual materials for shelving and racking were found inflexible and wasteful. What was needed was a new kind of construction material which would reduce expense.

The Dexion Slotted Angle was launched in 1947 and unlike many new ideas it was not a brainwave, but emerged from a deliberate search for an answer to a problem, an exercise in result getting. The problem turned out to be the evolution of a system of construction which would satisfy certain stringent requirements. It had to possess the utmost versatility and involve the minimum number of components, if possible only one. It had to be simple to erect, it had to be compact, it had to be cheap and there had to be no waste.

Only the users of the Dexion slotted angle will fully appreciate how well these conditions have been achieved. There is in fact only a single component yet this permits the construction of almost anything from a bracket to a building.

Today, the Dexion organisation is worldwide, with subsidiaries in Australia, Austria, France, Greece, USA, West Germany and an associated company in India, plus licensees in 18 countries from Chile to South Africa, Canada to New Zealand. It has a Head Office in Wembley covering approximately 42,000 square feet, and a UK factory at Hemel Hempstead on a 15 acre site. This factory is the largest in the world for the manufacture of storage equipment and the famous Dexion slotted angle. Production capacity at the highly mechanised UK factory alone exceeds 1 million feet per week, with more than 50 per cent of the output for export. With a wide range of products for storage and materials handling, building construction, steel flooring, display products and accessories, Dexion employs more than 1800 people in the UK alone.

Staff relations are considered excellent, the company is non-union and has never experienced a strike or stoppage of work. A recent poll conducted at the Hemel site revealed that 87 per cent of the labour force had no wish to join a union.

Demetrius Comino, the Chairman, took the lead in giving a series of talks to his senior management on the subject of job enrichment and employee motivation. While no one person or department is specifically charged with this function, throughout the company's 20 year history, a great deal of thought, discussion and application of ideas has been given to the subject of what motivates people and gives them job satisfaction. As a result, Dexion has gained a better awareness of the human need for growth and achievement, and a lot has been done towards providing the right atmosphere in which people can be allowed to develop.

Five years ago, the high turnover of head office secretaries and junior office girls became a serious problem. Mr Comino himself met a large cross section of girls in groups of five or six. After telling them that their turnover was high, he asked them whether anything was seriously wrong with the company and whether anything could be done about the problem.

He deliberately made it easy for them to say that it might be the inadequacy of rest rooms, canteen facilities and other general environmental factors which most managers considered to be the main reason for high turnover. Surprisingly, almost without exception, the girls dismissed these factors and were unanimous in agreeing that their main cause of discontent was boredom, and lack of interest and challenge in the work they did. What they wanted was more responsibility and this did not mean in charge of others, but rather the responsibility of making decisions and seeing a job through. On the whole they liked the firm, liked the people they worked with and the surroundings, but they got bored, and left largely for the sake of a change.

The secretaries considered their role should be that of anticipator, planning their time and resources to assist their respective manager. Instead they felt they were not much more than typing machines, accepting a letter to type and that was that. No indication was given of what the letter was about, the background, the reasons for its being sent and the outcome. The girls offered their complaints ranging from inadequate explanation of jobs, systems and procedures, to poor delegation resulting in under-utilisation of their skills. Many of the secretaries felt they had been hired to do a job which could have been undertaken by a competent clerk. One of the more important points emerging from these interviews was that there was little interest because there was no feedback of results.

The point was reiterated time and time again that working blind, without feedback of results, was considered a killing activity. One girl made a particular point of saying how much she appreciated having someone explain the whole picture to her, not only concerning an aspect of work, but also the company. The strong desire to feel part of the organisation was shared by many; they wanted to know more about the activities of the company, more about the history, its markets and its problems. Some girls suggested changing departments every so often as a means of alleviating some of the monotony of the job. However the general reaction was that it would be easier to change jobs, as many thought that their manager would be offended should they ask for a transfer to another part of the organisation.

Following the sessions of interviews the Chairman put into effect a programme of remedial action. Firstly, details of the interviews were circulated to all managers and senior staff. Each manager was asked to investigate his local situation, to take steps to improve matters and to report back on the action taken. He was encouraged to use his secretary more effectively, by giving her the background of a problem and a general outline of what was required, and by dictating merely the bones of a letter, leaving his secretary to get on with it and to follow it up herself. To keep her in the picture each manager was instructed to pass over any further relevant information following his secretary's action.

Over a period there was a noticeable change in morale and though there is far more to be done, there is simply no question as to the value of this approach. In fact, there was an immediate result since several girls who had been on the point of leaving changed their minds, and are still with Dexion-Comino International to this day.

Unfortunately, in far too many companies there exists the problem of high office staff turnover. Over-paying the secretaries did not buy their commitment, and as this company discovered, did not prevent them from going elsewhere when they became bored and disillusioned. Managers spend too much of their time supervising the job and the person, and too little time delegating tasks which frequently can be undertaken efficiently by their subordinates, in this instance the secretary. But it is essential to bear in mind my earlier comment: motivation, by itself, will not cure technical or clerical incompetence. People must have the tools of their trade to perform the task effectively. As serious and costly a situation as under-utilisation of a secretary is attempting to motivate an ill equipped clerk/typist to play a secretary's role. The junior office girl must be provided not only with the information she will require and the advice she will almost certainly seek, but also with the appropriate training she will need as a support to demonstrate the skills she already possesses.

With recruitment of a £12–15 a week clerk alone costing as much as £60 a head, and resignation within the first three months a further £120 in 'wasted effort', the under-utilisation of ability, the badly specified task roles, lack of personal achievement and depth of boredom in work loads are expensive factors. The enriching of the job to create more interest and more challenge, to offer more responsibility and opportunity for growth has in the case of the Dexion Group secretaries proved a profit making exercise in commitment and effort on the part of its managers. And far from impoverishing the jobs of the managers, the task delegation has left them with more time to encourage, to advise, plan and develop. In fact, more time to do more important work and make a fuller contribution to the company objectives. Who would want it otherwise?

Job enrichment within Dexion-Comino International has not stopped at the work role of the secretaries and office juniors. The second practical example concerns the design and development department senior workshop technicians of which there are three, with the shortest serving one having been in the department for nine years. These men are skilled toolmakers and work closely with the new products designers in engineering a product through in a practical sense. This is already a 'rich' job, in that a lot is expected of these technicians and they have ample opportunity to use their practical and creative talents in solving problems. They had all grown in their jobs over the years and their intellectual ability is beyond that specified in their original job descriptions. All too often job descriptions bear little relation to what individual people *really* do all day, however interesting they may be to read. However, about two years ago there was a detectable shift in their attitudes; a greater inertia against getting results was apparent. Attitudes and energies were slightly directed against the company rather than with it. The company and department had grown, and the technicians felt no longer as effective and important as they used to be.

A year ago their job was remodelled more appropriately to suit their deserved status, and a number of important changes were made. They were given staff appointments and paid a salary, thus breaking away from the company hourly paid structure, and allowing the Dexion Group to reward, more fairly, individual talents. They also now attend major new product development meetings instead of just 'working closely' with the designers of that department. They are involved at the beginning of a project and have the opportunity of contributing at the onset rather than being given a solution on a plate.

Three grades of development technicians have now been established, offering opportunity for growth and promotion in the job, and bringing their service and workshop status into a fairer balance too. They have been encouraged to deal with outside companies direct in working with an appointed sub-contractor. This change implied a greater responsiblity and, together with his being able to pass on to the sub-contractor the benefit of his acquired development experience, gave the challenge necessary for the technician's self-development. A further side effect of this was an increase in personal interest after the job went into production; there was a lesser tendency to say: 'That's somebody else's responsibility now'.

One Senior Product Technician said:

> 'I enjoy my new status and feel that it goes a good way towards where I feel I ought to be. Normally the only way I could reach this satisfaction would be through a Supervisor's function, but this way I have the status and still have the opportunity to develop things I enjoy.
>
> When the Senior Designer is away I deputise on all matters and my new status has given me a greater confidence. Now I prepare my own drawings, obtain quotations, work in conjunction with outside companies.
>
> All of these things were previously carried out by someone else. The impact of my work now spreads further, and I feel that I have earned more respect from my colleagues through getting results. I feel in a stronger position to put my own point of view and even to drastically alter the course of things.
>
> I get great satisfaction through taking on a loosely specified job and in helping people to make up their minds when they don't always know exactly what they want themselves until they see it. I feel that I have more freedom through fewer restrictions in the terms of my employment—and this gives me more personal confidence too'.

This case demonstrates an unsatisfactory existing position which has been changed to build up the job so that it became more complete in its own right and one which did not overlook the needs of the individual. As in the case of the secretaries, the job was organised so that the individual could see the results of his own efforts and the sense of achievement came over clearly. As much as possible was done to let the individual set his or her own objectives and have a greater, indeed a major, say in all aspects of the job that concerned the individual. The delegation of authority to make and take decisions offers the freedom necessary for professional growth. From the original situation of being under-utilised in the case of the secretaries, to having outgrown the job as with the technicians, the new job roles had become a learning laboratory, in which the individual had the opportunity for self-development.

It is interesting to note the work load of a Dexion Contracts designer. This position carries for each man the responsibility for a series of routine functions. One man is thus his own estimator–designer–project controller–erection supervisor and customer liaison man. Often the

49

more normal practice in industry is to give each of these functions to a specialist. Dexion have enriched this job for it was realised that each component function would be incomplete and lack interest. The separate parts were largely routine, and the essential element of a sense of personal achievement would be missing; that is to say on the smaller jobs, not to be confused with the team achievement and satisfaction on larger jobs. Further, feedback of progress on any particular job would be impersonal, and too much time would be spent on internal communications. Clearly, in the short run, it would have appeared to be perhaps more efficient to break the job down into its constituent parts, but in the long term giving the Contracts Designer more meaningful and less routine and boring work has paid off. There are about twenty Contracts Designers, one of the more senior of them having recently handled a job in Sweden worth £700,000. For an individual, £5,000–20,000 is quite a common responsibility. The staff turnover for this department is of a low order, and has a high stability index. Instead of being inundated with the communications problem which 20 project controllers, 20 erection supervisors, 20 estimators, 20 customer liaison men, etc. could bring, the important chances for responsibility, challenge and achievement have not been overlooked. The needs of the individual were considered right at the outset, when thought was being given to the structure of the contracts department, therefore it is difficult for me to compare a before-and-after situation.

However, the high stability rate existing with the Dexion Contracts Designers speaks for itself. And, with a satisfactory performance which results from the job itself providing the designers' individual development and motivation, again, who would want it otherwise?

case study three

Shell UK Ltd:

Stanlow Refinery

'There is considerable latent talent in industry waiting to be used if only the opportunity is given. Men are capable generally of doing more, much more, than management currently allow them to do. If only 10 per cent of this latent talent was released we might see a considerable change in our national economic fortunes.'

Derek W. E. Burden

Manager Micro-Wax Department
Stanlow Refinery 1966–68
now Consultant North Paul
Associates, London

I am extremely grateful to Derek Burden, Head of Personnel Research for Shell UK Limited, for his contribution to the details of the Stanlow Refinery Micro-Wax Department study and for giving much time and effort in describing the events within that department since 1965. Also for allowing me the kindest facilities within Shell UK Limited.
I would also like to acknowledge Peter Linklater, Personnel Director for Shell UK Limited for allowing the study to be published.

LKT, October 1971

It is necessary first to say something about the general environment of the Stanlow Refinery before looking at the specific problems of the Micro-Wax Department where this particular Shell study originates.

In the summer of 1965, the oil manufacturing function of Shell in the UK, with the assistance of the Tavistock Institute of Human Relations, set out to define its overall objectives and the underlying management philosophy against which they were to be achieved. The objectives of the company were defined in terms of its contribution to the long term profitability of the Royal Dutch/Shell Group and in terms of its responsibilities to society. The resources of men, money and materials were conceived as being fundamentally part of the total resources of society and consequently there was a responsibility upon the company to manage, protect and develop them in this light. Indeed, this social objective was seen as inseparable from the achievement of the long term profitability objective.

The philosophy was written down and it was considered that the business and social objectives of the company could best be achieved through use of the socio-technical concept of organisation. Readers are referred to the bibliography appendix should they wish to learn more of this concept of organisation, but basically it states that any organisation is made up of a technical system of plant and equipment, and a social system of people and their organisation.

The best results are achieved by considering the two systems together in a complementary supportive manner to achieve their joint optimisation less, possibly, than the optimum of either system viewed in isolation, but still the 'best fit' of the two together. The characteristics of the social system were defined mainly in terms of individual psychological needs in the work environment. This led to the conclusion that the social system in the joint optimisation process was going to require considerable assistance from knowledge of the behavioural sciences.

During 1965–66 some forty conferences were held involving refinery personnel from senior management to first line supervision to discuss the philosophy and objectives statement. By Spring 1966 the management climate in the refinery was such that new ideas and new methods, particularly in relation to the social system, were more readily accepted. This supportive management climate is most important if any attempts to innovate are to succeed, because it allows risk taking, without which most management ideas are still born. From the very beginning of this book I have insisted that for a fuller understanding of motivation, the first step is to understand the needs individuals have, and the second step must be the creation of an environment and the provision of incentives which will allow man the opportunity of maximising the satisfaction of all his needs.

Looking now more closely at the Stanlow Refinery's micro-wax

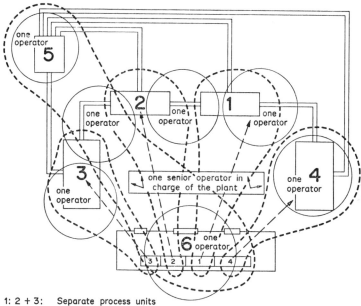

Number of employees : 28 established positions ——→ 6 operators x 1 shift
                        +4 relief operators   +1 senior operator x 1 shift

Note: 100% union membership TGWU

1: 2 + 3:   Separate process units
4:           Finishing unit
5:           Tank farm with 56 tanks
6:           Control (panel) room

Plant operators with original job boundaries
----- Plant operators with new job boundaries

Figure 3   Reorganisation of duties in Shell UK's Stanlow Refinery micro-wax department.

department, consider the illustration in Figure 3. With regard to its technical system, the plant up to the Spring of 1966 had been through a series of severe difficulties which appeared to stem from the enforced change to a different feed material from that for which the plant was designed. Pressure from the market had demanded continued operation from parts of the plant which were in need of overhaul and hence operating at less than maximum efficiency. This had resulted, of course, in lowered output, more pressure from the market, less time still for maintenance and so on—producing the inevitable spiral towards a complete shutdown.

The technical problems were magnified because this is the only plant of its type in the world and consequently all problems tended to be of a fundamental nature. The main problems were short term, practical, operating ones. The plant was producing at less than the market offtake and stocks being drawn upon for the balance were sufficient for only 6 more weeks. The only other source of waxes of the type required was in the USA and delivery time was 4 weeks. The general mechanical condition, and hence reliability, of vital parts of the plant was poor.

What about the social system within the plant? Morale among the plant operators was at its lowest. They had very little confidence in the equipment they controlled. Because of the serious market position the manager of the department had issued instructions that no alterations were to be made to plant operating conditions without his permission. This loss of control by those actually operating the plant led inevitably to some loss in their commitment. They had ideas on how matters might be improved but were not allowed to test them without reference to higher authority. As a result, few of the ideas were suggested and the plant supervisors, as well as the operators, were frustrated not only by repeated mechanical breakdowns of the plant and consequent long hours of work but primarily because they were not able to change the method of working.

Clearly, the only way to guarantee continued supply to the market and to avoid a shutdown was to order some buffer stocks from the USA. Due to the delivery schedule that had to be done within 2 weeks even if the plant ran well for the next 6 weeks. The stocks were obtained and, in so doing, provided a short term solution to the technical system worry at that time. What then had to be done was the injection of a will to win into the operators and supervision. This was to be achieved by involving them fully in the determining and commitment of the plan to recover from the serious situation confronting the plant.

The first departmental meeting was held in the manager's office with the plant senior operator, foremen and supervisor present. The senior operator was asked to hold a meeting with his shift team to pass on information obtained from the department meeting. The meeting examined many of the difficulties put forward by foremen, supervisor and senior operator.

A meeting was held every week, and gradually as the short term problems of the plant were solved, more general topics relating to the operation of the department were discussed. The meeting was later moved to the plant mess room where all the operators were able to attend, the supervisors taking turns to keep a watching brief on the plant. This expanded meeting provided the opportunity for joint problem solving rather than the indirect participation of earlier meetings in which the numbers had to be limited. It is worth mentioning that it was about a year after the venue was moved to the mess room before complete freedom of expression became apparent among the operators. So it was more than 2 years after positive steps had been taken to involve operators in the running of the department before the atmosphere was fully participative. And this in a management climate that was favourable. This point must be highlighted to give some idea of the time lag involved in behaviour and consequent attitude change. Attitudes cannot change overnight. As I said earlier the problems of frustration have been with us a long time and there is no quick, short term, easy solution.

The establishment of the weekly departmental meeting as an integral part of the process of managing the plant was the initial step in the growth of a participative style of management within the plant. Over the 2 years following this step other changes were introduced. Because of the layout and design of the plant, it was possible to organise jobs so that each operator had a complete unit to control including the instrument panel for that unit which was in the main plant control room. Doing a job which is complete in itself, making possible a higher degree of flexibility, fulfilling the psychological need for responsibility, these aims were satisfied through allowing the operator the opportunity for growth in his job. Each operator was encouraged to learn each of the four main process units so that maximum advantage could be derived from this opportunity for flexibility. Because the operators became experienced in operating the different types of unit on the plant they were good candidates for promotion to more senior positions on other plants in the refinery.

Operators experienced on one unit and now operating another unit on the plant were always willing to help less experienced operators during minor unit upsets. This feeling of competent back-up allowed training to continue even though the shift team did not have a fully flexible crew. This side of flexibility—work sharing to help colleagues out of temporary difficulties—was a most important facet. Without it job training and consequent promotion could not have been possible at anything like the rate achieved. Once again, we find people with latent skills demonstrating them once they are given the opportunity. The key motivator in all of these functions is growth, with the job being the vehicle of change and success.

Stanlow obtained flexibility within a shift team; flexibility across shift teams was quite another situation. The 'primary' group need that I explained earlier is often identified in a work situation with a particular shift. So much so in fact that even upon promotion or job change shift workers will often ask to stay on the same shift. I have encountered this in many industries, and the reasons for this are not difficult to find. The 'primary' group of the shift team often becomes a strong social group. They organise dances and sports activities together and probably most important of all is they often share transport to and from work. Therefore, to ask for flexibility between shifts is attempting to change a well established social order, albeit only temporary.

In order to allow free movement between shifts as required for training and sickness cover the senior operators of each shift were given the authority to cover as they themselves thought necessary. In order to facilitate this movement clocking was abolished, and the senior operators given the responsibility of recording absence. The presence of the time clock was seen not only as a deterrent to inter-shift flexibility but also as a lack of trust in the operators. Shift work is itself a regulator, time clocks being unnecessary.

This one move opened up many possibilities for the operators, and they took full advantage of them. The absence of the clock meant that they could come and go to some extent to suit their own social lives providing that they planned ahead and arranged relief cover with their senior operator's approval. This approval was given providing the replacement operator was competent, and continued safe operation of the plant was assured. This was done frequently and far from causing problems of administration it became a fully self-regulating system. When Everton played in the FA cup final of 1968, for example, no fewer than five men who would normally have been on shift attended and arranged their own cover—on a Saturday afternoon. The Department Manager learnt of the trip on the following Monday morning, and only then because of the result! Annual holiday cover became much simpler too because of the larger number of people who were able to cover.

The holiday rotas were left entirely to the senior operators to control. Only if agreement could not be reached would the foreman arbitrate— and he did this very rarely. The sickness absence figures for the plant have fallen steadily from 4·3 per cent in the Spring of 1966 to 2·4 per cent in 1970. Although it is not possible to pinpoint the reason, it is felt that with a cover system of the one adopted, absence became a more personal thing; one knew who was being inconvenienced, and this had something to do with the reduced statistics. More interest in the work and more department commitment in an atmosphere of responsibility and self-development are seldom an embarrassment. Absence and sickness are not only costly, as has already been pointed out, but symptomatic in many instances of alienation and withdrawal from the work situation, often resulting from job dissatisfaction, frustration and unnecessary general stress.

Another of the changes made concerned the operating log. Often continuous process work operators are expected to fill in record sheets concerning process conditions at set intervals of time. They often do not know why they record this information nor to what use it is put.

The time schedule for recording information is set, and seldom queried. The format usually suits the draughtsman and printer, and seldom is the recorder or user considered. An operating log sheet for the plant was designed in consultation with the operators which enabled the complete plant product position to be calculated once a day—at midnight. The operators themselves produced this balance and left the results sheets for the Department Manager and day supervision to analyse in the morning. One major feature of this log sheet was that records were required only every 4 hours, and then only on predetermined vital instruments. The emphasis was moved from the mechanical act of putting figures on paper to that of ensuring the correct functioning of the instruments and, if they did not, that they were quickly rectified.

The whole exercise of keeping information now had a purpose, seen and understood by the operators, and what is most important they could determine for themselves the results of their efforts once per day. The operator himself got the feedback, for he is the one who needs it in order to do his job especially when the responsibility for that job lies on his shoulders. To have information about the plant is one thing, but to have the authority to use it is a basic ingredient in the fuller participation that comes with job enrichment.

The senior operators had the authority to make alterations to plant conditions in order to meet the programme. This programme determined daily by the supervisor against the plan discussed at the weekly meetings was outlined to the senior operators. The programme was deliberately drawn up to allow the senior operators to exercise judgement, and they had the authority to exercise judgement. The process of change from an authoritarian system towards a participative one was most interesting to observe. For several months after the senior operators' authority to alter plant conditions was agreed, the Department Manager and other members of the supervisory staff were telephoned out of day work hours to discuss problems as seen by the senior operators. This was a most critical period for this was the period in which the senior operators were adjusting to the new way of working.

Invariably the telephone call was to confirm that action proposed was correct, although it was not often phrased that way. Often the problem itself was stated and the analysis of the situation, already made by the senior operator, had to be drawn from him. Refusal by the day staff to do any more than give advice quickly and efficiently when sought, information when required, is seen as a very important part of the development of the senior operators. They gradually learnt to use their skills, gain confidence and to seek assurance only when they really needed it. The telephone calls became routine reports of the state of the plant at the end of the shift. It was probably 6 months before this state of affairs was reached. Of course, some mistakes were made, but these were used to improve knowledge in order to prevent a recurrence rather than as disciplinary matters.

This is another example of management becoming a service, its purpose to provide the tools of the trade from advice to training, encouragement to support. Trust became and is a vital part of the recipe for delegation. Giving responsibility and the requisite authority to the senior operators, far from being a free-for-all in frivolity, demonstrated that the senior operators were perfectly capable of running the plant safely and efficiently, with its several million pounds' worth of equipment.

The senior supervisor's and day foreman's jobs were broadened by the added dimensions of financial responsibility. They were involved with the Department Manager in producing the operating budget and once the allocation of funds for their particular spheres of responsibility had been determined they were given complete discretion over the expenditure, with no control by the Department Manager—other than the commitment not to exceed the agreed budget figures! This financial control procedure is an example of a real, rather than apparent, attempt to delegate authority. Never to have left the shallow end of the pool would have seemed a safer situation, and one that is often sought by managers. But the delegation of authority and responsibility down the line to the supervisor with all the risks that it could have involved represents the concept of the supervisor as a first line manager, making use of the services available in technological, accounting and design departments in the performance of his job, rather than as an overlooker and an information provider for experts in service departments.

Let me turn now to the involvement of operators more fully in the running of the plant. There are a number of special instances which arose that indicate the extensive implementation of the participative approach.

In order to evaluate certain parts of the plant, for various reasons, test runs are arranged from time to time. For successful evaluation, it is essential that plant conditions remain as steady as possible and that samples and readings are taken carefully and at the prescribed times. The refinery practice had been for the technologist responsible for the test run to arrange for sample containers to be provided from the laboratory and then to take the samples himself. The argument has been that since the samples are to undergo careful analysis to be used in extensive calculation it is vital to have properly taken samples. In other words one cannot trust plant operators to take samples properly.

What was done at Stanlow's Micro-Wax department, in consultation with the technologist involved and the operators was to provide, with a short note from the technologist, information on the object of the test run. The need for accuracy was stressed while the rest—accurate recording of information, careful taking of samples and steady operation of the plant—was left to the operators. They were, of course, much more involved in the whole process and were much more responsible for its outcome. When completed, a copy of the test run report was left in the control room for the operators to read. It is interesting to note that these reports were the source of many questions by the operators on plant operation, and one suggestion made as a result of test run data by a plant operator produced a plant modification which enabled the plant to continue running a few months later when it would otherwise have shut down. This particular operator refused to have his suggestion considered for financial reward under the refinery suggestion scheme because he regarded it as part of his job. Maybe he was right; in any case I am told he is now a very good plant foreman.

As well as challenging the normal method of recording information on plant log sheets, the way in which samples were drawn for testing was also examined. Again, this is normally done against a set time schedule, in order that laboratory work may be scheduled. The disadvantage of this system is that it does not take account of the variations in plant conditions and as a consequence the laboratory results do not provide a sure guide to quality that one would hope for. There is also a considerable time lag in a large refinery in transporting the samples to the laboratory. An operator who takes samples at specified times is not encouraged to be involved with the result. And the time lag means that in any case the result is not often available until the end of his shift. To overcome both the time lag and encourage operator involvement, it was suggested that the operators might do much of their own testing on the plant. The rigid testing schedule was withdrawn and operators were asked to test when they felt it necessary in order to make on-grade product. It was found that during normal operation much less testing was done, but under abnormal circumstances much more testing was done. As a result doubtful material, which previously had run to off-grade storage until the laboratory results were available, was now checked frequently and put to on-grade storage much sooner, thus reducing the amount of reprocessing required. The results were that off-plant wax testing was reduced by 75 per cent and occasionally £100 reprocessing costs would be saved in one shift.

A scheme was devised by accounts department whereby the tank stocks were to be recorded on a form used directly as a source document for the computer. When this was first proposed to wax department, the operator controlling the tanks was the one who was asked for comments in discussions with the computer personnel. After examining the proposal form and listening to how the proposed system would work the operator himself suggested replacing the existing record form completely with the new form—and simply using a copy for plant records, reducing the excessive paperwork. This suggestion was welcomed and an explanation of the system was given to all operators controlling plant storage tanks. The effectiveness of this direct involvement is demonstrated by the fact that difficulties were experienced in some other departments in the refinery with computerised documentation of tank stocks, while in micro-wax plant the new system had a trouble-free introduction and escaped problems.

With regard to education and training, operators were positively encouraged to further their education in courses allied to process plant operation at a local technical college, partially in their own time. While this may seem only common sense, such positive encouragement is not always in evidence in relation to operator training, particularly in shift working industries where cover has to be provided for the absent trainee. The very flexible nature of the department's shift working system allowed this aspect of cover more easily than would have been possible under a more rigid system, and good use was made of it. Operators were keen to cover for one another for training purposes, even though in some cases they were obviously helping others to promotion ahead of them. This was another example of the team spirit generated as a result of the flexible working arrangements.

Because they were directly accountable for the performance of the operators working for them, the senior operator and day foreman were responsible for the ultimate choice of all operator replacements for the plant at selection panels convened for this purpose.

And so it goes on, for there are many other examples of job involvement and enrichment within this department. The encouragement by the management for ideas for improvement to the plant: to provide justification for the ideas and to develop these themselves, enlisting specialist help (drawing office, finance, technological) as required. Construction plans and commissioning were delegated with authority and this certainly helped to alleviate the frustrations that had existed in the plant previously in that positive efforts were being made to solve some of the technical problems—and principally by the frustrated parties. In no instance of the delegation did disaster occur; mistakes yes, but ones, as mentioned earlier, everyone learnt from and which were turned to good account at a later date.

The risks attached seemed formidable at first, leaving operators solely in charge of several millions of pounds' worth of equipment. Changes were made without pay demands, for the changes mostly were motivational in that they affected the psychological needs, those of challenge, achievement and responsibility. It was the reward of achievement that bought their commitment; it was the satisfaction with the task that bought performance.

The operators responded with caution at first, as in the example of the senior operators making alterations to plant conditions. They felt their way with their new responsibilities and sought advice and information from the service of management which responded with competence. As is illustrated in other studies, managers were left with more time for technical innovation, staff training and development and corporate planning. Given the opportunity, the operator demonstrated that his ideas were as good as or better than those considered by management in the case, for example, with the computerisation of documents. Subordinates were doing work previously undertaken by their superiors and were doing it as competently and more efficiently. Although it is difficult to express the financial gains the lower absenteeism, the meeting of output targets, the plant working at much nearer its maximum efficiency than ever before, the team spirit and the flexibility which cut down overtime, all speak for themselves. The output of each of the main process units has been increased considerably. In the first unit, output was increased by 35 per cent over the 1965 figure mainly by a technical improvement suggested by the supervisor at the very first department meeting. The finishing unit capacity was increased by 40 per cent over the original 1965 figure, again due to technical improvements many of which were suggested at the department meetings. In both these units, although the increases were principally due to technical changes, the understanding and knowledge which the operators had of the changes made played an important part in maximising the gains made possible by the changes.

The most important commitment to the job in hand, with resultant increase in output, was in the second and third units. It was important because this is the limiting section of the plant and output was increased 100 per cent; important because it is largely manually controlled. This part of the plant is extremely demanding because it has sixteen operating variables which must be closely controlled. Of course, the controls themselves are instrumented, but the interaction of the controls cannot be, due to the nature of the process. To optimise such a process requires knowledge of the operation, manual skill and constant attention to the job. As the output increases, so does the demand for attention to detail with the need for frequent minute adjustments to the plant. This is the type of job which can only be successfully accomplished by highly motivated operators—and the output increase indicated is a measure of the success achieved.

There is no doubt that provision of laboratory testing facilities on the plant helped motivation, because the operators were able to get immediate feedback on the results of their efforts. The job itself was fairly demanding both physically and mentally. The point is made again in this study by the operators concerned of the importance of feedback, and many times they said they felt they knew how well they were doing, and how much this encouraged them to go on. The whole unit appeared to be under their control. Surely this is just what Stanlow's micro-wax department was aiming for.

Ideally, of course, it would have been nice to have clean experimental situations with a 'before' and 'after' measure. However, the work was done as part of a continuous management process and not as an experimental project to test a management technique collected from the last London conference the department manager attended. Looked upon merely as a technique, such a participative approach would inevitably have failed. Participation is an attitude of mind and a mode of human behaviour opening the door to motivational change. It stems from a concern for, and desire to develop, human ability. For its future success, it cannot be used as a manipulative technique for securing the consent or support of the governed to a particular course of action. As a style of management which creates a new working environment leading to all the benefits I have mentioned in this study it has to be practised against a set of manifestly justifiable social values. Within Shell UK Ltd, the company's management philosophy fulfils this need. It implies more effective manpower planning. Many companies pay a great deal of attention to their financial and technical planning, as indicated at the commencement of this book, and to the working environment that makes up the 'technical' system. Never enough effort is given to the 'social' system planning.

The Shell UK Ltd philosophy and objectives specifically refer to the areas of psychological requirement of job content. The reader might like to see how the events I have indicated in this study fit these requirements:

1 The need for the content of the work to be reasonably demanding of the individual in terms other than those of sheer endurance, and for it to provide some variety.
2 The need for an individual to know what his job is and how he is performing in it.
3 The need to be able to learn the job and go on learning.
4 The need for some area of decision-making where the individual can exercise his discretion.
5 The need for some degree of social support and recognition within the organisation.
6 The need for the individual to be able to relate what he does and what he produces to the objectives of the company and his life in the community.
7 The need to feel that the job leads to some sort of desirable future which does not necessarily imply promotion.

Finally, to come right up to date, it is worth turning to the question of improved individual performance among the plant operators, and it is claimed that the department is a breeding ground of good senior operators. Generally speaking, refinery operating foremen are selected from plant senior operators, and micro-wax department has about 6 per cent of the refinery 'potential operating foremen population' of senior operators. From 1960 to 1965, 5 per cent of senior operators promoted to foreman came from the department, slightly less than the potential 'average' for the plant. In the five years since 1966, the figure has almost trebled, just over twice the potential 'average'. Once the pattern is set, of course, and people realise that such a mode of operation provides good promotional opportunity it becomes a self-generating system.

It is not claimed that total success has been achieved or that participation and job enrichment are universal panaceas for industry's problems. Behavioural change is a slow process as has been demonstrated earlier. In changing work attitudes and practices it is vital to do so slowly, gradually moving toward the desired behaviour pattern. Movement too soon or too much expected too soon can bring very strong reaction.

An example of risk taking and trust was the recent decision to purchase some new equipment for the plant, one piece to cost approximately £100,000. The foreman and supervisor between them drew up the operating specification required, entertained visiting technical representatives and, after showing them the plant, discussed their plans with them. Finally, they made the selection and it is the operating day foreman who will liaise with the manufacturers during construction.

This then is the present: a productivity deal has been concluded in the refinery and its introduction to micro-wax department has required the inclusion of a mechanical fitter into the shift team. This requirement was freely discussed at the departmental meetings and the best way of incorporating the fitter into the team was determined. As a result of this, the change to the new method has gone very smoothly and the shift fitter is now an integral part of the operating shift team. When the plant is operating smoothly he is an operator; when maintenance is required his operating duties are performed by his operator colleagues. The big point is that it does not represent a vast change to them, perhaps because they have been flexible operators for such a long time now! Elsewhere in the refinery such changes have not been so easily accomplished, another example of behaviour change being a slow and stressful process. As part of the productivity deal, abolition of the clock was confirmed and more operator flexibility required throughout the entire refinery, both accomplished some time ago in micro-wax department and not seen now as changes likely to cause an upset in the department.

Job enrichment is the specific building into an individual's job of the opportunity for achievement and recognition, challenge and responsibility, the scope for advancement and growth. This at the micro-wax department was combined with structural and environmental changes and married into the philosophy and business objectives of the refinery and company. In doing so, that company found out that men are capable of doing more, much more, and not necessarily with a price tag. If other companies adopted a similar philosophy and offered opportunities for satisfying an individual's needs, as outlined in the list of psychological requirements, then indeed might we not see a considerable change in national economic fortunes?

case study four

Mercury House Group

'As labour becomes too costly to waste, wherever possible, people should not only be given additional responsibility, but the opportunity to grow within jobs. They should also be allowed to acquire skills and knowledge which will make them an even more valuable asset to the organisation.'

Peter Gabe

Training and Development Manager
Mercury House Group 1969–71
at present Personnel Manager
Rocar Group Limited

I am extremely grateful to Peter Gabe for the long discussions we have shared on clerical training. I am also appreciative of the time and effort he has taken, while Training and Development Manager at the Mercury House Group, in providing me with many details included in this study, and for extending me every facility at the Group.

LKT, August 1971

The Mercury House Group is privately owned and employs approximately 900 people with interests in publishing, printing, wholesale and retail distribution. The Group has grown rapidly over the past 15 years and is now one of the leaders in the European trade and technical publishing business. The principal offices of the Group are in London with regional sales offices in Birmingham and Manchester.

The higher management control is in the hands of the Chairman and Chief Executive assisted by a group of divisional directors who, themselves, have senior executive responsibility for the operating companies. Late in 1971 the publishing companies and associated service companies were regrouped with the aim of coordinating their interests more effectively.

The principal characteristic of the Mercury House Group is the relative smallness in size of the various departments. The publishing companies are traditionally divided into editorial and advertisement sales departments with production personnel responsible for the collection and collation of editorial and advertisement copy.

In 1969, when a formal training function was established for the Group under Peter Gabe, attention was directed towards the activities of clerical and commercial personnel who account for over 50 per cent of total staff numbers. It was believed that these people represented a very significant cost factor, and concern was expressed by management at all levels as to whether the talents of clerical staff and of secretarial staff in particular were being fully utilised.

Initially, an activity questionnaire was compiled and circulated with the aim of building up broad job profiles. An analysis of these questionnaires soon revealed that many individuals were not carrying out functions which had been specified at the time of initial selection. Exit interviews revealed that, in several cases, staff were leaving because they did not consider that they had a 'real job'.

Many London-based employers are faced with an acute problem of employee wastage regarding clerical and secretarial staff as has been stated already in this book. However, the training and personnel specialists within the Mercury House Group believed that they should not be complacent about the situation and that positive steps must be taken to improve matters.

It was understood that job satisfaction and commitment come primarily from the opportunities, within the job content, of greater scope for recognition and personal achievement, responsible work and growth. It was hoped that the underlying concepts of job enrichment could be employed and that secretaries could be given a more challenging role with a greater degree of personal involvement.

An early step taken was to collate information on departments with a high secretarial turnover and to check on the reasons for resignations.

In many cases, girls considered that they had been misinformed at their interviews on the real job content and had been led to expect a more responsible position than was really the case. Among the secretaries I have talked with, the general complaint of being misled at the time of interview was held by many. It was not unusual to hear the girls say that bosses were usually lying through their teeth and doing a real public relations job for themselves. There was often a tendency to consider the secretary as a status symbol and not to realise her full job potential. This groan was often directed towards younger managers who felt that it was the 'in' thing to have a secretary when really the post didn't warrant it, and a competent clerical assistant would have served the job specification adequately. Often girls were hired as secretaries and then were concerned solely with routines and in many cases felt that they were considered as 'glorified clerks'.

As has been pointed out in another case study, the under-utilisation of ability, lack of positive career development, personal reward and satisfaction inevitably leads, as a number of companies experience, to the hasty departure of their commercial staffs.

In certain sectors of the Mercury House Group, a management training needs analysis was carried out and those who were considered to need formal training, especially in human relations skills, job specifications, employee selection, etc. were invited to attend a course so that problems could be ironed out. The prime criterion to be observed was that secretaries should only be appointed where the post really warranted it and that, otherwise, alternatives should be considered, for instance a shorthand typist or clerical assistant. The managers were also introduced to modern motivational concepts and, in particular, the work of Frederick Herzberg.

To condense Professor Herzberg's theories into a few sentences is to do him an injustice, and for a fuller appreciation of his investigations I would like to refer the reader to his works indicated in the bibliography appendix. Basically, from his investigations, it transpires that the work situations people find most satisfying and rewarding are those which provide the individual with the opportunity for personal achievement, and tasks which prove challenging and offer the opportunity for responsibility, advancement and growth. It is these features of any job that, in Professor Herzberg's studies, have been proved to hold the most power to motivate people to give of their best. It is this theoretical basis for job enrichment that the managers, not only of the Mercury House Group, but in many more of the case studies, have been introduced to in their training programmes.

Within the Mercury House Group, not only was the theory discussed but practical sessions and workshops were also included. Course members were divided into syndicates and were presented with the existing job descriptions of the secretarial staff. They found, as other case study companies did, that the existing job descriptions bore little relation to what the individual engaged on the task actually did. Many times, a 'dilution' of the job was occurring. By limiting the requirements of the job level to fit the minimum capabilities of the job holder the chances of error are reduced. But, it also discourages those with higher abilities from doing the most efficient work in their assignment. A diary approach to the job description is probably wiser: an analysis of work over several weeks is more likely to show features which cause difficulty or involve an undue investment of time. Once this analysis was done, the course members were asked to restructure jobs to give a more challenging content and responsibilities. This was felt to be a valuable exercise for, as I pointed out earlier, the staff of any one department is relatively small and any work which could be undertaken by secretaries, enabling their managers to concentrate on more pressing matters, would be helpful. On other occasions, groups of executives were formed to discuss any possible increases in the job responsibility for their subordinates, whether they were practical or impractical, and these were subsequently refined as to their feasibility.

This motivational 'brainstorm' session is always part of any job enrichment programme. Initially the changes discussed usually concern those factors in the *outer* circle of Figure 2 on page 31, but subsequently develop into discussions relating to the *inner* circle, that is the motivators.

Particular interest was shown in duties which would not only provide new responsibilities but would also require training in new skills and knowledge. Industry has largely neglected secretarial training and there is a real danger of obsolesence for this category of staff. The furthest that many firms are prepared to go is to instruct in departmental procedures, assuming that all secretarial training has been adequately covered either at school or college. On the other hand, formal management training is considered, by many companies, to be an essential part of job experience. This can best be illustrated as:

	Before employment	*After employment*
Managers:	Hardly any training	Formal induction and development
Secretaries:	Training abdicated to colleges and schools	Some induction, very little training

I would now like to elaborate on the provision of new responsibilities and increased skills that were acquired by secretaries through the job enrichment programme.

Increase in job function: Attending press conferences.
Increase in skill required: Training in reporting techniques.

Many secretaries in editorial departments spend a considerable amount of time copy typing and filing. They were hardly involved in the real work of the department and many complained that they were on the 'touchline' of operations. On the other hand, members of the editorial team were inundated with invitations to press conferences which they could not fulfil and so the assignment of certain visits to secretaries was considered beneficial.

This gave the secretary a deeper insight into the industries with which her journal was concerned, and with the personalities about whom she had only read beforehand.

A reduction in supervision was considered vital and therefore the individual secretary was given total responsibility for the authorship of the report of the visit. The management support for this change came in the provision of the specific training in techniques of reporting and this, of course, was undertaken in company hours.

Increase in job function: Writing all business letters except the Manager's personal letters.
Increase in skill required: Training in letter writing techniques.

Before the job enrichment exercise, managers spent a considerable amount of time dictating or even handwriting routine letters which it was felt could be adequately delegated to the secretary. The secretary's training tends to make her an expert in communications skills and particularly in writing effective business correspondence. Now the girl would not only deal with all correspondence but, in many cases, would sign them herself without reference to her manager. Verification or checking was completely abolished and the secretary would only refer to her manager if she needed clarification or information on any point. Management again supported her with the provision of adequate training to cope with this increase in tasks.

Increase in job function: Dealing with advertisement copy.
Increase in skill required: Knowledge of the technical aspects of publishing.

Advertisement managers were often over-engaged with routine queries about the quality of advertisements which prevented them from devoting as much time as possible to selling activities. Secretaries, after being given adequate training in the requirements for good copy could now deal with these queries themselves. This brought them in direct contact with the advertisers and enabled them to gain an insight into the technical aspects of the publishing business. On-the-job training, not only by their managers but also by the service function of the various printing processes, gave the secretaries an appreciation of both the practical aspects and technical terminology involved in the production process.

This informal link between the secretary and the service function also 'enriched' the job of the latter, as he was now given the opportunity to teach his skill and felt a closer link with the 'white collar' side of the business. Likewise, the opportunity of offering the benefit of their technical expertise was given to the manager, as he was responsible for teaching his secretary the requirements for good copy.

Increase in job function:　　Sub-editing press releases.
Increase in skill required:　　Training in précis writing and British Standards.

Each day a considerable number of press releases land on the editorial desk and staff spend much time on rewriting these releases for inclusion in journals. A competent secretary can take on the responsibility for going through releases and for being accountable for their sub-editing. This job encouraged a more independent and indeed professional approach to her job, for not only did the secretary have now direct contact with management on the respective journals but she was also responsible for specific topics. As she alone was accountable for the sub-editing there seemed to be a increase in the degree of self-supervision, which was more thorough, and not as frustrating, as the verification by a superior. As many of the Group's journals are of a technical nature the girl again gained a deeper insight into the nature of the industries. Also she extended her knowledge into the field of terminology and, in particular, the skill in translating manufacturers' measurements into British Standards (BSI).

These are examples of attempts made by the management, in conjunction with the personnel and training function, at providing secretaries with more interesting and worthwhile jobs. A typical new job description is shown in Figure 4, in this instance for the secretary of a Production Manager. The enrichment of the subordinates' jobs has, as is also the case in other studies, resulted in a chain reaction, with superiors' and other individuals' jobs also being enriched.

The relatively routine work of copy typing and filing became a challenging job for some of the clerical staff. The routine work of queries on advertisement quality became a responsibility and challenge for the Advertisement Manager's secretary. These individuals were now doing things which had previously been done before by more senior people and were, with training, doing it as competently. As has been indicated in other studies, this kind of involvement is the key to motivational change, being the kind of involvement that occurs only through the fuller participation possible with job enrichment.

JOB DESCRIPTION

JOB TITLE: Secretary/Production Manager
JOB HOLDER: Christine Howe

Department/Council
Section: Ad.

Approved by: *W. H. Whyton*   Effective: 25/2/71

I. FUNCTION: Responsible to Ad. Manager (B. Whyton) for the smooth running of the office and all routine duties involved.

II. RESPONSIBILITIES:

2.1 Deals with all in coming correspondence.
2.2 Takes shorthand notes and types all letters, memos, reports etc.
2.3 Deals with routine enquiries by telephone.
2.4 Filès all correspondence, orders and enquiries regarding advertisements.
2.5 Organises department's stationery.
2.6 Works out and types weekly reports.
2.7 Types monthly report.
2.8 Monitors competitive journals.
2.9 Acknowledges all orders received and sends details to the appropriate reps.
2.10 Enters all orders received into record book.
2.11 Keeps up-to-date diary for Ad. Manager.
2.12 Responsible for office equipment.
2.13 Supervises Trainee Production Clerk/Secretary.
2.14 Responsible for ensuring collation of copy by specified date.
2.15 Ensuring that invoices and revenue sheet are accurate.
2.16 Responsible for training Production Clerk/Secretary to achieve working knowledge of copy procedure.
2.17 Responsible to Ad. Manager on all matters concerned with magazine production.

III. AUTHORITY:

3.1 Composes, types and signs routine letters in Ad. Manager's absence.
3.2 Authorises extension of copy dates.

IV. RELATIONSHIPS:

4.1 Advertising Agencies.
4.2 Birmingham Office.
4.3 Manchester Office.
4.4 Editorial Department.
4.5 Printers.
4.6 Block Makers.
4.7 Clients.

Figure 4 A job description for a manager's secretary with enlarged responsibilities, in the Mercury House Group.

I mentioned in the earlier part of the book that the 'downward communication' system giving information and advice was a basic factor satisfying a person's need for security. It does not however motivate that person; the only person motivated is the one giving away the information, advice and ideas. But in this study, as in the others, there has been no discontinuance of consultation, as managers have still communicated their information and advice. But the difference is that the information and advice were sought, asked for; it was a two way system involving consultation upwards as well as downwards. And this at the instigation of the subordinate. Both the manager and the subordinate were motivated. The manager was encouraged because of his need to ensure that his staff were properly equipped to cope with the responsibility of the increased task load, to satisfy himself that they received the appropriate training—in fact, the accountability for their career development.

The motivation of the subordinate is evident from the studies, examples being the authorship and accountability for the press conference reports and all business letters within the editorial departments. Other instances were the greater degree of self-supervision, in that verification and checking of the reports, letters and in the sub-editing of press releases was either minimal or totally abolished. There was more involvement in the work, not only regarding the nature of the industry, but in the direct contact with clients as when dealing with the advertisement copy. There was more dealing direct also with line management and service functions as occurred in both the sub-editing and advertisement copy duties.

There was greater involvement too in the organising of work loads, in being able to select the priorities of press release or the reply to a client's letter. The opportunity was presented for professional growth as accountability for the job in hand lay on the shoulders of the subordinate.

Not only had the manager the responsibility for his staff's career development, but he had to be competent at providing the information and advice when sought, for example in the study of secretaries writing all business letters and signing them except in the instances when they required technical advice or clarification. The managers also shared a greater responsibility in the recruitment and selection of staffs and often for this they themselves required training.

Therefore training programmes not only included the encouragement of new techniques and the acquiring of human relations skills, but also interviewing procedures, recruitment and selection education and performance appraisal. They also had to learn how to draft job requisitions in order to combat the over-recruitment problem, since recruiting a highly qualified person, superior to the requirements of a job, and then under-employing her on routine tasks aggravated the problem of clerical and secretarial turnover. The routine secretarial work became a challenge to the clerical assistants and junior shorthand-typists. Thus a logical approach to their on-the-job training, as well as the requiring of advanced skills for the secretaries, became the subject for discussion at the managers' training school.

It is very difficult to express the gains of job enrichment in any financial term, but certainly there is tangible evidence of reduction in employee wastage. Not all girls, of course, welcomed having their jobs enriched, and lack of interest, when it did occur, came from those girls who probably would have left the Group anyway even if things had been left the way they were. Certainly good secretaries always jumped at the new job opportunities, and often poor secretaries instead of remaining poor developed a real enthusiasm. Certainly nothing was lost or got worse. The new jobs offered opportunity, never demand; the gauntlet was either picked up or it was not. But, because managers too were adequately trained to provide a strong and competent supporting role, the girls were more likely to swim than sink.

And from a secretarial labour turnover figure of 61 per cent in October 1969 the figure a year later read 48 per cent with a downward trend continuing in 1971. The clerical figure of 66 per cent now reads 45 per cent. If one just takes the recruitment cost of £60 a head, without taking into account a 'wasted effort' figure if the girls say 'I'm leaving you' soon after arrival, then the savings are considerable if turnover can be reduced as much as 20 per cent.

It is difficult to measure the financial gains yielded by managers' work being now undertaken by someone else lower down in the organisation. Certainly, the checking and handwriting of reports and letters were superseded by the managers, in some instances, having more time to sell, and at all times having time to develop their own skills as well as those of their staff. The vetting and verification, once the chore of the manager, became the challenge for the subordinate. Allowing managers and subordinate alike to acquire skills and knowledge, and to positively encourage their individual contribution to the company objectives, can only make them an asset to that organisation. Can such a valuable asset be an embarrassment?

case study five

Carrington Dewhurst Group:

William Tatton and Co Ltd

'A man on a Coventry assembly line who is allowed 0·23 standard minutes for grasping, locating and tightening a bolt in a body shell, presents a social problem which cannot be solved by further analysis, training and the application of more cash. Yet this same man as a consumer is expected to be so discriminating that he will buy a Terylene/Cotton shirt rather than a Dacron/Cotton shirt with which it is chemically identical. We encourage him as a consumer to be creative, to experiment, to inform us about his ideas and preferences. But when this same man comes to work we expect him to switch off and buckle down.'

Stephen Johnson

ex Managing Director
William Tatton & Company Limited
now Joint Managing Director
British Enkalon

I am grateful to Stephen Johnson, ex Managing Director of William Tatton & Co Ltd for providing many of the details necessary in order this study could be compiled.

I am also particularly grateful to Brenig Williams, Group Personnel Director for discussing the study and providing every facility on my visits to Leek.

I would like to acknowledge Anthony Marchont, present Managing Director of the company, for allowing me to publish the study.

LKT, March 1971

The Carrington Dewhurst Group employs approximately 17,000 people, and the Group is divided into four major divisions: garments, warp knitting, yarn processing, filament woven which also includes dyeing and finishing activities. The Group manufactures a whole range of textile products, including such items as dresses, suits, raincoats, shirting, underwear and ladies' tights, as well as certain heavier end products such as tarpaulin and balloon canvas. William Tatton is part of the yarn processing division, employing 2500 people. The yarn processing activity is located at four sites in North Staffordshire and South Lancashire, and produces single filament texturised yarn on cone and beam for the knitting and weaving trades. Its production is sold both to customers within the Carrington Dewhurst Group and to independent manufacturers outside the Group.

The business philosophy of this company, like any other, is that which has been found to work, to produce results in terms of building an organisation of men and machines that creates wealth. But what works at the optimum in one day and age is unlikely to be the most appropriate method of operations in a later era. This because, not only will our knowledge of techniques have changed, but also the nature of the society the business organisation seeks to serve. Many of the case studies have established that what is an appropriate business approach in 1971 is not just a question of training our management in the latest techniques but also of making them aware of the social environment both inside and outside the company, within which such techniques must operate. As mentioned earlier society is in the grip of yet another revolution, be it automation, computerisation or classroom. The pace of technical innovation and change is influencing all our lives in more and more immediate ways. William Tatton realised that our ability to create wealth has freed us from most of the laborious time consuming chores that prevented freedom for thought and leisure pursuits. This fact, together with higher standards of education for all of us, have radically changed the nature of opinion and attitude in contemporary life. People now bring greatly increased expectations to their work place, not only in terms of increased earnings, but as a source of interest, challenge and experience. Therefore, the business philosophy that Tatton's have aimed to develop is one that can contain such expectations, not in a negative sense of keeping everyone happy, but in a positive manner by matching expectations with opportunity within the company organisation. In other words, the company have to capitalise on improved human resources and set them to work.

Just as society as a whole has changed, so has that microcosm of society—the company. Our present state of knowledge and general approach as to what makes people tick has altered since Taylor's principles of scientific 'work study' management, which demanded more or less that man be regarded as a part or appendage to his machine—a static element in a production process, to be kept oiled and greased by way of punishment or reward, but never to be allowed to be moved one fraction out of step with his machine. This Ice Age of scientific management was gradually modified in the thirties and since by the growth of a body of knowledge now known as the behavioural sciences and the application of such knowledge to the problems of managing an industrio-commercial organisation. This case study presents an opportunity for me to explain by way of example such developments in management practice.

William Tatton took an early interest in the dyeing and, later, in the processing of synthetic yarns, but the decade just past saw its major expansion through an involvement in the new methods of processing man-made fibres. These methods demanded an increasingly high capital investment in the machinery required, and this fact, plus the enormous demands for products like nylon and crimplene, necessitated 24-hour working and almost perfect machine efficiency if a return on capital was to be assured throughout a boom period. This assurance was guaranteed through the techniques of work study and various forms of planned maintenance. Production methods and flow patterns were analysed and the process operator's job broken down into its nth element by the work study people. Training programmes for the operatives were devised on the basis of such analyses and payment-by-results systems introduced using the work values they established.

It cannot be denied that the result was a far more efficient production operation. It will always be a primary task of business management to observe, analyse and reorganise methods of collection, production and distribution. But wherever the work study specialists make the assumption that by offering increased financial reward to the human agents in a production process, productivity will automatically occur, they are in error. And this, unfortunately, is the tacit assumption payment-by-results systems seem to be based upon. The responsibility for this may not be the work study practitioners but this misapplication of industrial engineering techniques must be restrained if the proper use of analytical data is not to be increasingly curtailed as workers become more discriminating.

I would suggest that where a work situation is restructured as a result of the application of work study, increased efficiency and a higher productivity may result not only from the reorganisation of the work methods and the opportunity for the operatives to earn more, but also as a result of the fact that there is something new in the employee's working life, and that management have taken an interest in his existence even if only through the recording of a stop watch. This suggestion seems to gain credence when one observes the fate of payment-by-results systems over a period of years.

The operative becomes accustomed to the Work Study Officer, he learns quickly exactly how much effort will be needed to produce earnings of a desired level and contrary to the expectation that each individual will continually strive for the maximum bonus, he decides what his most comfortable earnings level is and then achieves that regularly week after week. Union negotiated increases in basic wages ensure the operative's earnings remain in line or even climb above the rise in the cost of living. The result is a standard of living most employees find tolerable and the demise of the idea that increased human efficiency will occur in line with the opportunity for higher earnings *alone.*

As the contents of this book have reiterated, other factors are involved in deciding how much time and effort an individual will devote to his job, that money does not buy commitment. It is on this score that the behavioural sciences are becoming of increasing relevance to the problems of modern management and are of prime importance in developing a company philosophy and an effective work force. It does make sense in terms of increased productivity if we treat people as people— creative, imaginative and with wishes and desires peculiar to each individual, rather than as parts of a machine some of which do not work as consistently as the other parts. All the studies confirm that it is only work which is personally rewarding that will produce the interest which is necessary if a job is to be discharged with competence consistently. Any role which allows an individual to make a personal contribution, however small, or which allows a sense of achievement, in any sense, is the only way in which interest and continued commitment can be engendered. The rewards of personal satisfaction and achievement are earned and are the elements in a job that fire enthusiasm, create a sense of commitment and involvement, much more so than the traditional rewards of salary, fringe benefits and status. I must repeat that these latter mentioned rewards have not diminished in their importance; if anyone feels underpaid he will be just as unhappy with an interesting job as with a boring and monotonous one. The shift of emphasis relevant to management is the appreciation that a person will still be dissatisfied even if he is extremely well paid, if his job does not allow him to achieve satisfaction of all his needs and carry a sense of personal responsibility.

It was therefore considered to be a critical part of the Tatton company philosophy that looking at the jobs the individuals were doing would pay dividends. That analysing, measuring, defining tasks, methods and operating standards, calculating areas of accountability, authority and discretion has its limitations. Of itself, it cannot provide the means of overcoming the problems of automated drudgery. Instead the employee should be encouraged to participate in developing and conducting the

business. He should be given the opportunity to regulate his environment in a way beneficial to the community, to advance personally
through his enterprise and ingenuity, and generally be allowed to participate in change by being permitted to change things. As these studies
show, where this liberating approach is adopted productivity improves
and goes on improving.

Tatton's decided to attempt to restructure the work, not on the basis
of principles laid down in work measurement, but on the basis that
trusted employees will enjoy and wish to accept as much responsibility
and personal authority as they are capable of establishing. An initial
pilot project with their shop floor was in the Mayfield Mill. This mill
employs about 450 people of whom 50 are staff (monthly paid) and the
rest hourly paid. The mill is engaged in winding continuous threads of
man-made fibres onto large beams, which are then sold to customers
for use in their knitting and weaving operations. There is a full range
of jobs at Mayfield mill, varying from the most routine domestic
factory chores to the semi-skilled operation of winding the processed
yarns onto a beam. Three different production areas were selected for
the project, and three different types of approach were made in an
attempt to enrich the work.

First the coning department:

Here yarns, after processing, are wound onto packages suitable for use
in fabric manufacture. The operatives are mostly female and are responsible for one or more banks of machines performing the coning
operation. The operatives were divided into work groups of about 20
people and one operative was selected as a 'team captain'. Her work
load was reduced and the uncommitted time available during her day
was used in a number of different ways. For instance, team captains
began by completing a rough attitude survey. Complaints and grievances
which were endemic in the attitude of employees, and which for various
reasons were not mentioned to management representatives were
quickly brought to the notice of the departmental manager by the team
captains. The nature of these reports were educative in themselves.
Grumbles about pay and conditions of service while present were not
paramount, but two other factors were. Firstly, oblique references to
the nature of the supervisors (both men and women), that is personal
relationships: and, secondly, comments on the efficiency of the plant:
whether the machines were clean and adequately maintained, whether
supplies of yarn were delivered as requested in the correct quantities
and so on. The importance of creating conditions in which the job can
be properly performed was very evident, and the group leader (team
captain) idea seems to have scored a success on two counts. Firstly, by

providing a direct means of communication between employee and management, and, secondly, by stimulating a sense of commitment and involvement on the individual's part as to what went on in the department.

The second area of steaming and coating:

The operation involved steaming each cone of thread to stabilise the twist put into it elsewhere in the factory. This was followed by applying a coating to each thread that prevents clotting and tangling of the thousands of separate threads during the subsequent operations. It is a small department of six employees and one supervisor, half the men worked in the steaming section and the other half in the coating section. The work was reorganised by training all the men in both steaming and coating and allowing them to tend a job lot through both processes. In addition, the day to day administrative work of the department was broken down into individual parts, so that each man became totally responsible for his weekly load as allocated to him by his supervisor. Not only did this allow the men the opportunity of extending their skills but, of course, allowed for greater job flexibility in times of absence, training, etc.

Warping department:

The operation in this area is fairly skilled, with the job requiring a great deal of patience and an incredible power of observation in picking out the odd loose end or defective thread in the thousands of ends being wound onto a beam. There was one supervisor to every six or seven operatives, and this supervisor organised the supply of materials, maintenance, work planning and allocated the service labourers (known as creel loaders) who set up the supply of threads in large racks that are then run into the beam. The technique used here was to delegate as many supervisory responsibilities as possible onto the shoulders of each operative. Each person then became responsible for his or her own communications with other departments such as the maintenance area, store room and indeed other production departments supplying the processed threads for winding. In addition, each operative took charge of a team of creel loaders for the period they were required to set up the supply racks for the winding operation. The last, and perhaps most important feature of this restructuring, was the introduction of a weekly production meeting attended by the operatives and chaired by the department manager. The purpose of this meeting was to advise each operative of the total work load for the department for the coming weeks and to plan each individual's work as a part of the whole. This identified the targets of the individual not only with the group and department but also with the company objectives.

As with the team captains in the coning department, the meetings in the warping department gradually extended in scope to include general reports which ranged from the state of morale to quality control problems. But the fully participative atmosphere that accompanied the extension of the topics at these meetings took time to develop. As indicated frequently in other studies, the process of behavioural change is a slow one, and the long history of frustration that accompanies the imprisonment of ideas and expression cannot be liberated overnight.

What happened to the supervisors? These attempts at job enrichment liberated them from the day to day administrative rubber-stamping chores of running a shift and, in so doing, provided a small group of skilled, experienced men and women for a fire fighting role. For instance, the skill involved in the winding operation is such that an extensive period of on-the-job training is required before an individual is capable of operating on his own. One supervisor was immediately re-deployed into a remedial training role supporting those operatives not considered able to fulfil the job of an operative after enrichment. In fact, all the supervisors now had time to do things which were never properly done before, if at all. All of them played a fuller management role with regard to training and forward planning, and certainly they found the task of supervising people who were committed to a job and who had authority and responsibility in demanding work situations, much more rewarding than controlling robots.

From these experiences, Tatton have learnt a number of points that could well become indicators as to the future conduct of their industrial relations. They have uncovered and made available to management a knowledge of their production methods which could only have come from the people intimately involved with the methods on a daily basis. They have found that management, once their support has been enlisted, are the best qualified to map out programmes of job enrichment, and in so doing have retained the initiative in their management of labour. In time, Tatton hope that the greater fluidity in the line structure of management that followed the programmes of job enrichment changes outlined will also result in an easier indentification, promotion and training of management potential. In creating an atmosphere in which emphasis is placed on what each individual is *willing* and *able* to achieve rather than on which union he belongs to, job enrichment may well become an aid in solving such thorny problems as work demarcation and craft qualifications.

Job enrichment is not something confined to the shop floor. It is something of use, perhaps at its greatest, in creating conditions for managerial effectiveness in the upper echelons of the managerial pyramid. Much remains among large as well as small concerns of a paternalistic attitude to middle management on the part of chief executives and their Board colleagues. Paternalism takes many forms, but it is characterised by an elaborate attention to most generous fringe benefits of all forms, coupled with a rigid centralisation of decision making among a small number of men. Such management seems to view their employees rather as the American settlers viewed the Red Indians—as children by nature self-centred and consequently irresponsible, but not to be held in blame for such characterisation, for after all they knew no better. Success in such a managerial environment depended upon accepting a well defined job and performing in it conscientiously for the next 40 years!

Companies immersed in the lessons of job enrichment such as William Tatton, on the other hand, tend to throw emphasis upon good communications, the maximum amount of participation in business decisions, a less rigid attitude to defining individual's work loads and a corresponding accent on the team effort involved in all company activity. But the proof of the pudding as always lies in the eating. Such an approach might produce chaos in a company by its lack of rigid individual control and its assumption that men wish to demonstrate their responsibility and abilities. Its justification lies in the way this style of management corresponds to what people expect or would like to experience in their working lives, and in so doing reaps a harvest of enthusiasm and taps a wealth of experience and knowledge. As an example, let us consider the graduate.

The graduates often enter industry completely untried in any commercial sense, and unaware of the standards by which they will be judged from then on. But they also bring expectations, both social as well as in terms of job content, that tend to unfit them for 95 per cent of the jobs available. The result in some companies is a rapid turnover in the early years of graduate employment born of frustration, disillusionment and anxiety as to his future success. This is confirmed in the undergraduate survey I discussed earlier in the book.

If a company is to adequately utilise such highly trained, intelligent manpower, it becomes a question of providing a series of roles that will integrate them into the life of a company. Obviously, if that company's organisation is rigidly pyramidal and its style of management authoritarian, the problem will be more difficult. If each person has been allocated a neat pigeonhole, the very process demands a regimentation that can only produce job contents consisting entirely of administrative routines. If job enrichment can provide jobs that require intelligence and initiative and not just stamina, as indicated in Shell UK's company philosophy, then that company has gone some way towards meeting the problem of absorbing any person with an individual contribution to make. If the fuller participation generated with job enrichment can produce an atmosphere in which it is easier to gravitate from one side of a business activity to another, it would make easier the task of developing these all-round entrepreneurial managers that many companies require so very badly.

This company discovered that such organisational flexibility also allows an easier approach to those tragic cases of managerial obsolescence. The usual origin of such inability to know what is required of one has been a slow stagnation over many years in one position. Promotion seems to have passed the manager by, he deals with the same problems year after year, afraid to attend a training course in case the extent of his own supposed ignorance is revealed, and terrified lest such attendance should diminish his status. An across-the-board reorganisation of job contents that a programme of job enrichment entails often provides the opportunity of allowing such men to find a new level of responsibility or perhaps an entirely different function. And this in a far less painful way than, for instance, job rotation where one or two individuals are singled out for movement, and where it is all too apparent that only the young men hope for promotion and only the older men fear demotion as a result.

Job enrichment will also uncover a man's hidden talents or ambitions: so often the line structures in British industry do produce situations in which a more able subordinate is blocked in his career progress by a less able superior. Such instances are a bonus, but the reverse may also occur. Managers whose jobs have been changed also find that the criterion for a successful performance has changed, and some managers presumed to be highly competent performers can be revealed as highly competent 'yes' men who have cultivated the 'nice guy cult' until it has become their only management technique.

Tatton's have discovered that approaches such as job enrichment and management by objectives that demand each individual to analyse his own personal contribution and allows his organisational position to be determined by that contribution, can be most revealing and at times cruel in their effects. For the implications of a job enrichment programme are far reaching. It demands an analysis not only of one's employment policies, their recruitment and selection techniques, but forces a consideration of the types of specialist skills that a business requires. For example, are that company's managers providing the right type of leadership? Is the organisation adequately ordered to encourage rather than discourage innovation, whatever the source of that innovation?

Everyone is fully aware that the pace of technological change makes success not only relative but also extremely temporary. In fact, the

Tatton company realise that change itself appears to be the sole constant. If man's genius is to innovate then the only hope for continual success is to allow him to innovate and react on every possible occasion. As in the case of the coning department with the female operators, the comments of paramount importance to these operators concerned the job itself. Removing restraints, the management opened the road for improvement and admitted that they had uncovered a store of knowledge on their production methods which could only have come from the job holder.

In the steaming, coating and warping departments, responsibility was passed down the line resulting in the operators themselves being accountable for the weekly work load and for the requisitioning of various services and materials. The reduction in supervision not only encouraged the operators to have more direct contact with other departments, but allowed the supervisors themselves to develop their own talents and to acquire and use the fuller managerial role.

It is therefore obvious that this company has reaped much talent by encouraging the participation which comes with job enrichment. This has involved laying more stress upon informal patterns of relationships and structuring the formal organisation around such patterns. It has meant working through informal committee rather than through formal command. It was carried out on the basis that when all else is defined in a highly regulated environment, then the only time employees can apply any ingenuity is when they are working to beat the system and not the objectives. And on the understanding that participation would fail if the management never left the shallow end of the pool, for example, merely humouring their work force temporarily by appearing to solicit their ideas when there was no real intention of using them to alter the way the business was run.

It became part of the company philosophy that only if people had an opportunity to work creatively, to do more interesting work and to have prospects of further advance would their performance levels raise. Was this company not recognising the real state of affairs anyway?

case study six

Electricity Board

'There is a need for management to think in the long term to find a radically different approach to the problems of personnel management. Proper work processing, layout and organisation are essential, but we must discover ways and means of stimulating people at work to produce more. Tinkering about with pay—while inescapable—is only part of the job. Man is much more than a machine, we have to consider him as a human being and feed him with the correct human relations food. Otherwise starved of an outlet for his personality, the worker will wreck the most careful organisation, ignore the tools, materials and methods, and sabotage production by introducing restriction on output.'

William Walsh

District Administrative Officer
The Electricity Supply Industry

I am grateful to William Walsh and the Electricity Supply Industry for supplying me with many of the details related to this study, for giving me every help in its compilation and allowing it to be published by me.

LKT, April 1971

This Electricity Board has one and a half million customers, each taking a supply of electricity and each requiring different services according to the agreements—such as maintenance of apparatus, installations, hire purchase, etc.—they enter into. To provide these services, maintain technical information about the Board's equipment on customers' property (for instance meters, fuses, phases of supply, voltage, etc.) and render correct accounts, simple but accurate records are required. A record card exists for each customer. Prior to the introduction of a computer, these records were usually set up on 8 by 5 inch cards of standard design and maintained manually in each 'district' office by a group of clerks. The clerks originated instructions for work to be done and then amended the records to show the results of that work. The number of clerks employed depended on the number of customers in the 'district' which is usually from 20,000 up to 120,000. The organisation pattern for a district had evolved rather than been planned, and in the main the staff establishment provided for three levels of supervision above a group of general clerical staff. This is shown in Figure 5.

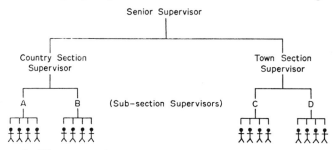

Figure 5   *The pattern of organisation for clerical workers in a district of the Electricity Board.*

Each sub-section consisted of one 'chargehand' and three general clerks. Each sub-section looked after about 30,000 cards. Within that sub-section, the chargehand looked after about 3000 cards, the clerks 9000 each. The functions of each level of staff were, very broadly, as set out below.

> SECTION SUPERVISORS Dealing with all correspondence emanating from consumers; answering all specialised and difficult questions; replying to all correspondence; liaison with industrial staff supervisors about hold-ups on work; dealing with problem matters (for instance account reference allocation); staff training arrangements; checking on performance and work position; verification of accuracy of recording; allowances; liaison with other sections and departments.

INTERMEDIATE SUPERVISORS (SUB-SECTION) Clears stoppages in work flow; checks on the work of the clerical staff; reporting to his section supervisor on progress; signs standard letters; maintains production of statistics; dealing with specific matters of technical routine (for example HP queries, quoting prices for new house services, etc.); allocating consumer reference numbers in liaison with meter reading staff; actioning meter reading reports; maintaining stocks of forms; cash posting queries.

CHARGEHAND Job training; allocation of clerical work; taking over vacant positions at times of absence; processing 'on-the-spot' queries; telephone liaison with customers.

CLERICAL STAFF Routine preparation of operational orders and updating of information on the record cards on the receipt of completed documents; initialling of boxes on operation orders to show the work completed; movement of copy orders to show progress of originals through the departments.

These arrangements and job functions were traditional, worked well and organisational and method checks had not suggested that any major improvements could be made. Even up to date management advances suggested there was little in the short term that could be done to improve the fixed clerical procedures along the lines of the job functions indicated. The introduction of the computer caused a major change. The size, type, nature and layout of forms changed. Routings were altered and much of the statistical information previously manually produced became normal computer output. Record 'cards' gave way to computer prepared and automatically updated record sheets. The routine raising and preparation of several types of operation order was done by the computer. In fact, much of the previous preparatory work of clerical staff was eliminated, while the amount of processing and verification increased.

At the same time as this major change was taking place, work study techniques were being applied to the office. More scientific data enabled judgements to be made about what numerical establishment was required to cope with the new work loads emerging with the advent of the computer. More important, the process of work study defined more closely the some 60 different jobs that had to be performed in a consumer records section and gave details of their magnitude.

The major change involved the cooperation of accounting, secretarial, administrative and management services staffs of districts and headquarters to programme work, edit manuals of procedures and envisage the outcome. The process contributed materially to understanding the human relations aspect of the work and the need — if accuracy and high outputs were to be secured — to make the job interesting and challenging, rather than routine and dull. In effect, six basic criteria for job enrichment were employed:

1 Extending the boundaries of the individual's responsibilities by adding to his duties others naturally associated with them.
2 Concentrating the more technical jobs and creating more specialists to do them.
3 Giving the individual more freedom to set his own objectives while increasing his accountability for what he does.
4 Reducing the amount of supervision to which individuals are subject.
5 Creating natural units of work and giving the individual more authority to make decisions within that unit.
6 Introducing more challenging and exacting jobs (perhaps previously handled at the supervisory level) accompanied by the requisite training to handle them effectively.

A study of the newly emerging jobs in the district offices resulted in a decision that the intermediate level of supervision should be eliminated and that the main supervisor's responsibilities should be restricted to taking over those difficulties which grew too large for clerical staff to handle. Certainly, the scope for reducing the verification and duplicate checking of the work was enormous. The supervisor once freed of this job would have more time to concentrate on the training of his staff, reviewing performance records and the long term development needs of the department.

So the new job was visualised for clerical work improvement and for staffing levels on the basis of the whole job lying with the clerk, this leaving the supervisor to cope with the time consuming managerial role indicated above. The new organisation pattern for the district became:

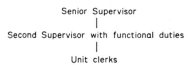

Senior Supervisor
|
Second Supervisor with functional duties
|
Unit clerks

Broadly under the new arrangements:

1 All telephone calls and mail flows directly to unit clerks.
 All specialised and difficult questions also go in the first instance to them.
 It is only when they cannot cope with a query or the advice given by the supervisor fails to produce a result does the question go to the supervisor.

2 They write and initial their own letters to customers, and are given training to write human and understanding letters.

3 They liaise directly with industrial staff supervisors on questions of held up work and the design of work programmes.

4 They prepare credit and refund documents. These are subject to query by the supervisors, but the accuracy of the calculations are entirely the clerk's responsibility.

5 They deal with semi-technical queries arising within the group of customers for which they are now responsible.

6 They initial all standard letters.

7 They deal with special arrangements, such as banker's orders, Giro payments, calling on the computer for print-outs, puzzle out and correct rejections from the computer.

8 Initiate action on meter reader reports.

9 They report on their own work load direct to the supervisor.

In every sense, this has been job enrichment in a situation where the use of work study techniques has guarded against mere job loading by establishing reasonable work quantities. Each clerk deals with a group of customers, roughly 10,000, and becomes, as it were, their representative and contact man with the Board's organisation. To many, the introduction of the computer often results in the subtraction of an individual's contribution to a job, but in this instance the management used the major change resulting from its installation to see what could be added to the job content.

The unit clerks now regard themselves as an élite corps and competition for training is high. The new job function had attracted good (7/8 'O' level type) clerks from banking and once trained these return and 85/95 level of performance. The training process now takes 6 months from rudiments of data processing to business letter writing, a much more challenging job for second supervisors. There is greater pride in the work, clerks taking care in their correspondence and relations with customers. They accept the responsibility without question and are much more committed to the job. The phrase which continually comes over is 'Interest and care in their jobs'. The job is no longer a boring and defined routine clerical procedure. It has become many sided, because it is now a challenge, the doer achieves an awful lot of satisfaction which cannot be taken away from him. Another comment is that 'time flies'. Interest in the job is so sustained that clocks and calenders certainly are no longer of prime importance!

What about the supervisors? Certainly, the boundaries of his job responsibilities are extended and they have latched on fairly quickly to the much more exacting training required for the staff, both new staff and the old, some of whom had difficulty in digesting new ways. They had to become computer-minded to ensure that when approached for advice on technical problems from the clerical staffs they provided the information with competence, and communicated it with ease, thereby earning the respect and confidence of their subordinates.

As in other case studies, it was discovered that control of the job was no longer a matter of 'on-the-job' supervising but more a means of providing the correct management support by providing the tools of the job to the holder; advice and information when required, more ambitious training and keeping an eye on the level of paper on the clerk's desk.

They have more time to devote to better forward planning, to the possible sources of improved customer service and to other jobs which are so time consuming that either they had not been done in the past, or not done properly. Certainly, the fear that supervisors previously held, that the delegation of their job roles to a subordinate would result in lower standards of work and in redundancies of supervisors, were groundless. For the chore of checking became a self-supervision challenge to the job holder, thereby allowing supervision to become a 'management service'. Supervisors now have time and confidence to undertake more important tasks in meeting the objectives of the organisation.

As important as the training responsibility was that of selection, finding the right man or woman for the job. One of the results, for example, of the computerisation of the clerical job was the production of many 'pianola rolls', or tabulations showing the present state of affairs in respect of consumers' accounts, etc. These tabulations, in turn, and when properly understood, show what jobs need doing in order to reduce costs, or eliminate sources of future consumer dissatisfaction. Broadly, the original idea was that each tabulation should pass through the hands of clerks, each one dealing with about 10,000 accounts.

In fact, it was found that some clerks grasped the message of what action was needed on different tabulation much more readily than others. So it followed naturally that 'tabulation Kings' emerged, each expert in a particular line of action. Instead, therefore, of each clerk being chivvied into expertise, the 'kings' are used as specialist interpreters. They point out the job to which *urgent* attention is needed and leave the remainder to be dealt with in a routine fashion. This change in job function satisfies a number of criteria, one being that the sense of achievement felt by the specialists becomes very much more enhanced. It provides an opportunity for promotion for the non-specialists who aimed to become a specialist themselves. Also, freeing the non-specialists from some of the tabulation tasks, allowed them more time and responsibility for on-the-job training of new staffs entering the working units. The result has been a much happier and more efficient working office, and a much more satisfied supervisor. The satisfaction of supervising responsible people with challenging and demanding tasks is much more rewarding than verifying the automatic clerical procedures that accompanied many of the tasks in the supervisor's original job function.

To younger and more adaptable staffs who can take change in their stride, job enrichment has been a stimulus. Once their field of responsibility became clear and the limits defined, they enjoyed the job and produced a higher standard of achievement than anyone would have forecast. However, older staffs more bound by years of the traditional organisation pattern and way of working found the changes more difficult to cope with. The problem is not that they cannot see what is intended, but that they cannot get used to the idea that someone is not continually checking what they do. The fact that they do not have to refer to the supervisor but can have a shot at the problem themselves takes time to penetrate and become accustomed to. Nonetheless, they were helped in their acclimatisation by the support of the management, with their supervisors making concerted efforts towards training, communication and establishing confidence.

The feeling by the management was that, initially, overall performance had a tendency to dip. It was difficult not to get panicky at this stage, but it was merely the learning process taking place. As it proceeded, efficiency rose slowly but it took as long as 12 months before it really blossomed. This perhaps explains why when talking to the senior levels of management during that period they appeared to have more qualms about the programme than, say, the section supervisors, whose anxieties stemmed mainly from a not uncommon resistance to change. Many held personal views about the job enrichment programme and said, often in other words, that it did create more job satisfaction, did encourage and spur them to greater efforts. It was felt generally that the long term benefits appear to be:

1 More contentment and agreed higher morale in the 'enriched' sections.
2 Less supervision, and lower costs, without deterioration in the standards of work.
3 The development of a better attitude to the job and much more recognition of the importance of good customer relations.
4 Staffs themselves say they have a better sense of participation in really worthwhile work, and often feel a real and lasting sense of achievement.

This demonstrates how the six criteria mentioned earlier in the case study were satisfied when restructuring the jobs in the clerical section following the introduction of a computer. Job enrichment has not stopped at this and the management are continually looking at the jobs individuals are being asked to do. Just as pay and working conditions are reviewed, so must the job itself.

Taking the first criterion mentioned, that of extending the boundaries of individual's responsibilities by adding to his duties others naturally associated with them, it might not seem, for example, that the job of a meter reader could be enriched. But it has been done. They were (and are) often the recipients of the housewives' confidences about the state of their electrical equipment, and their desire for new or improved gadgets. Busy housewives do not always have time to go into an electricity showroom and therefore the hearer of a grievance is often the meter reader. So the meter reader is given a brief form on which to report that 'so and so is interested in such and such'. The report is routed to specialist salesmen and if a sale results the meter reader is told and paid a small 'incentive' bonus. At regular intervals, they are brought together to tell management and discuss with them what it is that customers find irritating, or how the consumers feel about the service they receive. Management respond with ideas and plans for improving the service and the meter readers provide suggestions. This 'confidence sharing' brings its rewards by adding interest to what could be a very dull routine task, and by involving the individual in a genuine decision making process.

Another criterion of the 'human relations' policy is that of giving the individual more freedom to set his own objectives while increasing his accountability for what he does. Removing some of the mystery and nonsense which often accompanies management by objectives, one secures acceptance of ideas and targets by consultation with the people who have to carry out the job. This throughout the works right down to the matter of cleaning and the cleaners. A comparison of the results procured by outside cleaning contractors with those of the Board-employed cleaners was — to put it mildly — not flattering to the latter. 'Idle so and so's', said the supervisor responsible.

The cleaners were brought in one evening not to clean, but to discuss the job itself, against the background of what cleaning contractors offered to do for their money. What transpired was not that the cleaners were idle, but just badly organised, trying to do too much at once. The more talk that went on the clearer it became that the cleaners were doing some jobs daily which could be done weekly and some weekly that wanted doing daily. Some equipment and materials were deficient or inefficient. 'Okay, okay' said the supervisor, 'you draw up your own cleaning schedule, and subject to agreement by me, make out your own orders for the things you feel you need to do your job well'.

Certainly, the cleaners' idea of a cleaning bill is now *less* than it used to be, and the place sparkles more. The office and works residents no longer complain, the cleaners are much happier and 'take greater pride' in the end result of their labours.

This is another example of subordinates doing a job previously undertaken by a superior and doing it better and cheaper. Cleaning requirement ordering previously undertaken by a supervisor was now delegated to the persons actually doing the job. Being held accountable for the targets they themselves set has engendered a challenge which is not inherent in the job of many office cleaners.

Another yardstick mentioned was that of reducing the amount of supervision to which people are subject. At one time, a particularly busy service office was manned by five operatives, who rarely left the telephones in front of them. Two supervisors were considered necessary to sift the incoming jobs, decide the order of priority for attention and deal with the awkward customer who believed his job alone was all that should be accorded attention. As the operatives became more experienced, management decided to reduce the supervisors from two to one and to give the operatives more responsibility for deciding on priorities and for contacting by radio-telephone the men in the field.

The first results were not good. Management had not provided the operatives with the tools of their trade. The operatives were not trained sufficiently in the identification of most urgent calls, nor were they fully aware of the traffic difficulties the men in the field had to contend with. The cure for both these weaknesses lay in sending the operatives out with the service staff. The field force and the office based operatives built up an *ésprit de corps* and identity of purpose. To the operatives concerned it was much more satisfying to be able to give callers not the answer the supervisor calculated, but the one they knew for themselves to reflect the true work situation. Having actually been 'out on site' themselves they were able to deal in a much friendlier and more common sense way with the customers. This restructuring also satisfied the criterion for the introduction of more challenging and exacting tasks, after the requisite training to handle them.

A consistency in all of the restructuring of job contents is to be found in the two way communication process that is necessary. Cleaners, telephone operatives and meter readers were all approached, and instead of being presented with a *fait accompli*, were asked for ideas on the subject. The popularity of horse racing, football pools, newspaper competitions, quiz shows is not solely based on getting something for nothing, but more on the challenge of solving 'problems'. Encouraging employees, therefore, to make their own decisions, to solve the problem for themselves far from being adopted as an 'in' management technique has been accepted as a natural common sense development of the job.

As mentioned earlier, there were the sceptics as well as the enthusiasts and they now wonder what all the worry was about. They have experienced for themselves, like the night cleaners' supervisor, that people were capable of doing more, much more, than they were ever given credit for. In summary, it is fair to say that individuals responded cautiously at first to their new responsibilities, especially with the older established employees. However, they felt their way, sought advice and intensive training, which met with a response from management. It was the jobs individuals were doing that bought their commitment and the comments of 'time flies'.

On a routine clerical production line, it was originally difficult for supervisors to assess who was and was not happy with their lot. It was difficult to judge who was and was not stretched and which individual had more to contribute to the organisation. Once categorised as an 'ordinary' clerk it tends to become a static judgement, and this is the very bad circle that job enrichment breaks. Performance appraisal could now be undertaken in its most genuine sense. For the programme saw some clerks remaining the same, many more being satisfied and accepting the improved job content and the emergence of the specialists (for example 'tabulation Kings') whose hidden talents the restructuring uncovered. Suddenly the moronic task had become demanding, and presented the job holder with the opportunity for growth, increased skills and a promotion prospect that was a reality.

As other case studies have endorsed, at no time did disaster occur. Opportunities were accepted or they were not, and in the majority of instances individuals swam. In many of the instances, individuals who were considered as a prospect for possible sinking, surprised their superiors by swimming better than many of their colleagues. This was, therefore, a compliment to the management decision, and one that should be stressed when considering a job enrichment programme, not to make the restructuring changes selectively. The new job opportunities in the studies I have indicated were available to *all*. Thus, when individuals were well appraised and promoted, like the 'tabulation Kings', it was in recognition of their achievement at having swam *better*, but having had their performance judged over an equal distance.

And the results were there for all to see, from an improvement in clerical efficiency and morale to the reduction in the cleaning bill. Upon review, would the organisation ask for it otherwise?

case study seven

Swedish State Power Board

'We realised that to install a system which was an improvement on the old one, was not enough; the people affected had not been involved in the process of designing the change and so were uncommitted to it. When we had another attempt, this time involving the people concerned, not only did we gain commitment but in addition, arrived at a better technical answer than before'. Bo Widergren, *Head of Organisation Department, Swedish State Power Board.*

I am grateful to Mr Bo Widergren and the Swedish State Power Board for allowing this study to be published, and to Alan Wilkinson of ICI Dyestuffs Division, for providing me with much of the detailed information. There is further reference to this study in *A Survey of some Western European Experiments in Motivation* (Alan Wilkinson) issued in 1971 by the Institute of Work Study Practitioners.

The formation in 1965 of a special O & M function within the organisation department provides us with the background to this study. In recent years, this O & M group have been involved in a programme of simplifying and streamlining the administrative work of the Power Board. The first stage in this programme had been carried out in a fairly standard way, applying O & M techniques to the more routine, repetitive administrative tasks, which were easily defined and measured and which traditionally respond to such an approach. However, it was realised that this type of work only accounted for about 10 per cent of the administrative costs of the Board. Consequently, if significant inroads were to be made in improving administrative efficiency, some way would have to be found of tackling the more complex, variable kinds of activity.

The particular case study I am going to mention concerns the work of the buyers in the head office purchasing department which may be roughly classified as belonging to the middle level of administrative work in terms of complexity and responsibility. The investigation was triggered off by a work flow problem. To understand this problem it is necessary to know something about the organisation structure of the purchasing department at that time. Briefly, the structure was a traditional hierarchical pyramid, with a Purchasing Manager, five group-leaders and five groups of buyers. This is shown in Figure 6.

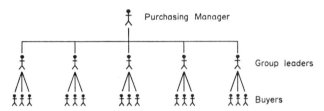

Figure 6   The original hierarchical structure of staff in the purchasing department of the Swedish State Power Board.

The five groups specialised, being divided up on a 'type of material' basis; for instance one group would deal with steel fabrications, another group with tools, another with cables, etc. In theory, the group leader was an expert on all aspects of his particular group's work, and each buyer had a more limited knowledge of the work within the group, varying according to training and length of experience.

The problem was one of fluctuating work loads, caused by seasonal variation and the peaks and troughs which resulted from, for example, the various stages reached by major construction programmes. The effect of this was that the Purchasing Manager found himself having to arbitrate daily on moving buyers from one group to another on a temporary basis to cope with local peak demands or absences. At seasonal peaks, overtime was very high and in fact, over the year, over-time averaged 10 per cent, which was leading to high costs and morale problems. This situation finally triggered off a request by the Purchasing Manager for permission to increase his establishment of buyers by two. In order to support his estimate of requirements, the organisational department was asked to carry out an investigation into the work flow problems, and assess the real manpower needs of the purchasing department. In this investigation, a twofold objective was agreed:

1 To increase productivity, which in the purchasing section included improving service to clients, and buying at favourable prices, in addition to volume-to-buyers hours ratio.
2 To increase the level of work satisfaction in the department through involvement and the fuller participation that was considered to come from job enrichment.

The first step was to obtain some factual information about the work loads and the fluctuations in the work load. This information was obtained by carrying out activity sampling for the whole staff during a 1 month period, which generated standard data for various classifications of purchasing operation. This data was then applied to historical records, to give an assessment of work loading and variance.

The result was surprising, for the department's work load could in theory have been undertaken with *fewer* people than were then employed. After further investigations, it was agreed to devise and install a planning and objectives system which would make more effective use of the human resource available, and which would also smooth the work flow. In addition, alternative methods of work were to be considered, and one of these alternatives chosen. It is interesting in the light of subsequent findings that at this stage the generation of alternatives and the choice of one was not carried out in a 'participative' fashion, despite the stated objective. It was very much a 'decide and sell' exercise.

The organisation chosen was as follows: the Purchasing Manager would control five branch buyers (the former group leaders) who would be specialists in various fields. These branch buyers would *select* the tasks which most required their special skills and knowledge; the remainder would be routed through a Planning Manager who would report to the Purchasing Manager. The Planning Manager would allocate these less complex purchasing tasks to a group of general buyers using the standard data previously obtained and a simple flexible planning board. Figure 7 illustrates the new organisation.

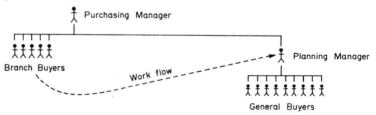

Figure 7   The reorganised structure of staff in the same department.

In economic terms the results of the first change, which was completed in 1968, were:

1 Virtual disappearance of overtime.
2 A *reduction* in staff which, against the business volume handled, is equivalent to a 30 per cent increase in productivity (a saving of approximately £25,000 per annum).
3 The number of complaints and 'forgotten' orders have been reduced to a minimum as a result of the efficient planning system, which naturally has led to much better relations with client departments.
4 Analysis of records has shown that the quality of buying (i.e. price achievements) is as good as, or better than, that for the original organisation.

Economic results were therefore good, but this was not so true on the social side of the account. Achievement against the second objective was apparently not so promising. An attitude survey was carried out in May 1969 and it produced the following results. The general buyers were unhappy because the branch buyers 'picked out the plums' from the work. Three of them felt stressed by the use of standard time for planning. In fact, despite the disappearance of overtime an attitude of mind was created by the use of planned times which made them feel as though they were operating within a piece work system. Previously no targets had existed, 'work to completion' being the rule.

This disturbing discovery of low job satisfaction triggered off a further investigation, this time in a more participative mould. From the introduction of monthly discussions with the buyers, dissatisfactions in addition to those above were identified, which included personal relationships, an unsatisfactory information system, the fact that the same standard time was always applied to the same job, regardless of whether it was being done by an 'expert' or a 'general buyer'. There were also the payment anomalies for there were no financial rewards for demonstrated productivity increases. In fact, the disappearance of overtime had meant in practice a *drop* in earnings. We have seen in another study that the concepts of a productivity bargain while simultaneously cutting the earnings rate is a speculation an employee is deaf to. There was a general unhappiness existing among this group of employees, but perhaps the greatest factor of dissatisfaction was inherent in the new organisation. It was felt that the new organisation had assumed that the only people with specialist knowledge were the former group leaders. Yet, each buyer had his own expertise, which was not being recognised or used. There was, therefore, not only the concern for recognition of ability but similar disquiet regarding the opportunities present for self-development.

Talking privately with two of the general buyers, they confirmed the dissatisfactions identified during the monthly discussions and also highlighted the following points. All the buyers had been upset by the *method* of introducing the changes: a sort of 'Here's our new plan, any comments? Well thanks for your attendance. The new plan comes in on Monday'. In the new system, continuity was lost, since a general buyer could be handling one type of purchase today and another tomorrow. The branch buyers had already reiterated their unhappiness about losing their supervisory role but the general buyers too also felt a loss of status, for they had become 'jacks-of-all-trades'.

On the credit side of the account, however, there was strong support for the planning system, with general agreement that it made much more effective use of people's time. During the period since the change they felt that things had improved and the introduction of monthly discussions on the organisation and tasks were thought genuinely participative. They stated that their views had been fully expressed on these occasions and were taken into account and acted upon.

The outcome of this participative review phase of the second objective was a recommendation reached by consensus that the organisation should be further changed. It was thought that there should be *one* group of buyers, all of whom should be subject to the planning system, and all of whom should have some degree of specialised responsibility. Status of the more senior buyers could, it was thought, be maintained by differences in grading in salary level within a job evaluation scale. This suggestion to senior management has now been accepted, and

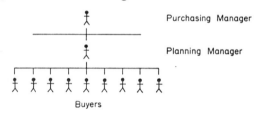

Purchasing Manager

Planning Manager

Buyers

Figure 8   The final staff structure after further discussion and experience.

from talking with the buyers it seems certain that most of the outstanding dissatisfactions have been removed by the implementation of these recommendations, in the second phase of the programme of change.

The expected results of this improved organisation:

The economic gains indicated by Figure 8 are hoped to be maintained and in some instances increased. Also the following advantages appeared:

1   *All* work can now be planned. The Planning Manager can allocate work to special skills and experience across the whole group thereby

acknowledging that *every* buyer has some field of knowledge in which he is the 'Group's' expert. Targets can now be more accurately set and individual feedback ensured.

2 Any rivalry and animosity that existed between the 'branch' and 'general' buyers has been removed, and it is hoped that this will evolve much more of a 'team' spirit than existed previously.

3 The new organisation should now allow some continuity of work to take place for each individual, in order that he can increase his knowledge of his special subject.

4 It now avoids the suspicion that the 'branch' buyers are 'picking out the plums' before passing work out to the 'general buyers', which was an original grievance revealed from the attitude survey.

In addition to this, the original advantages of the planning system for a flexible group have been retained, and in some senses, increased.

This case study represents an example of 'work structuring' not being used in any pure form. It was an integral part of an O & M exercise used to tackle a real economic problem requiring a relatively short term solution. It was an efficiency improvement exercise along established lines but taking into account the breadth of up to date knowledge on the behavioural sciences and job design. The philosophy was always one of opportunism: 'Since we are having to make changes anyway let us improve the human system at the same time as the technical one'.

The reaction to the process by which the first change was reached is important. It is difficult at times to choose the right place on the scale which ranges from 'tell' to 'sell', from 'consult' to 'involve'. The choice depends on many factors such as the time available for reaching a decision, the culture of the organisation as experienced both by the manager and the subordinates, the ability of that subordinate to play a useful part in reaching a decision and so on. However, in this case, the follow-up discussions and monthly meetings made it very clear that the original decision had been arrived at by a process too near the 'tell' end of the scale. The second recommendation for change (the 'one big group' idea) was agreed to have been generated in a much more involved and satisfying way. In this context, it is especially interesting to record that this 'one big group' idea was in fact one of the alternatives generated by the original management studies. Moreover, it was seen as being the best solution, but was *not* used on the grounds that 'it would be impossible to sell it to the buyers'! It might be as well to remind the reader here therefore that the process by which a decision is reached has at least as much effect on the success of any resultant change as the quality of the decision. A technically good decision, to which the people who will be affected are uncommitted, stands little chance of success.

One of the grievances which were indicated at the monthly meetings was the inadequacy of an information system, which could set clear goals and provide feedback to the individual on his performance against the goals. This is another example of working blind without feedback or recognition being a killing activity. There was also the common fallacy that a group leader possesses the sum of his subordinates' knowledge and experience when, in fact, it is more often the case that each member of the group, including the leader, possesses some latent skill or knowledge which is not present to the same degree in any other member.

Each person has now been recognised as an expert in his own right, able to do a complete job and be held responsible for the contract. The monthly discussions, the more efficient planning system and objectives setting keep everyone well informed on the targets and achievements within the department and, individually, also allow for the promotion of ideas and suggestions on the task loads and methods of working. The new method of working on the 'one group idea' will allow the Purchasing Manager more time to devote to long term planning and training of the buyers as opposed to sifting through and distributing the purchasing tasks and other rubber-stamping and red tape chores. As the vetting died so new, higher, orders of responsibility were born, namely that of long term planning and an accountability for training. The scope for self-supervision among the buyers was increased and the challenge to gain additional skills was apparent, providing even greater scope for personal achievement.

Job enrichment has been married into the structural changes that a new technical system often demands. The setting of objectives allowed the aims of work and the individual to be considered and helped create not only the economic results mentioned earlier, but a level of job satisfaction that had been hoped for in the original second objective of the organisation department.

Experience has proved to be the only way of discovering the skills the purchasing department personnel possessed, and diagnoses of future problems can take into account this experience. This may prove to offer a much wiser and profitable solution to a problem than taking a mere analytical approach.

Having recently returned from SSPB I discovered that the concepts of planning systems and project groups had been extended to other parts of the company with a similar history to the events in the purchasing department. A great deal of this now occurs at the secretarial and clerical levels within the company and benefits experienced have been felt with the same satisfaction as within Case Study 2—Dexion-Comino International. Job enrichment within the SSPB has now become a way of life and is considered an important union-management function. It is as strong in this company as others in Sweden (see Case Study 9—The Volvo Group).

case study eight

Volkswagenwerk AG

'Every one in Volkswagen knows we're not selling the most powerful car in the world, the most beautiful or the most economical car in the world. But everyone knows, right from the beginning, the thing we're selling is quality. The responsibility for achieving this quality is placed squarely on the shoulders of every working man. This accountability contributes to the dignity of the workers which, in the opinion of the unions, is as important as his wages and working conditions.'

Herr Reimer Siemsen

Vertraunsleute
(man-of-confidence . . . shop steward)
Volkswagen – Wolfsburg

I am extremely grateful to Volkswagenwerk AG Germany for providing me with every facility and assistance in the compilation of this study and for allowing it to be published. In particular, I should like to acknowledge the help received from Claus Borgward, Director of Quality, Hans Herbert Lembke, Vice-President of the shop stewards, Herbert Schlipper, Member of Personnel, Social & Wages Department. Also Rudi Maletz, Foreign Press Officer, and Dr Juan Wulff who provided instant translations in three languages and Herr Siemsen, who with fellow shop stewards, introduced me to German industrial relations and tolerated interruptions to production in the compilation of this study. Finally I am grateful to Philip Stein of Volkswagen (GB) Ltd, who succeeded in getting me to Germany whilst BEA were on strike, and my return to UK when Lufthansa had followed suit.

LKT, October 1971

Not for bread alone

After visiting Wolfsburg in Germany in 1949, a postwar British Commission representing the British motor industry reported that the Volkswagen Beetle did not meet the fundamental technical requirements of a motor car. Their report went on: 'As regards performance and design, it is quite unattractive to the average motor car buyer. It is too ugly and too noisy . . . a type of car like this will remain popular for two or three years—if that. To build the car commercially would be a completely uneconomical enterprise . . . .' The Wolfsburg factory of VW which had been offered to the occupation powers, was subsequently turned down as being 'virtually worthless and of no competitive concern to our own motor industries'.

That was in 1949 when the British turned over the control of the factory to a trusteeship representing the Federal Government, the state of Lower Saxony and the company employees at that time numbering approximately 8300 wage earners and salaried staff, contributing to a yearly production figure of 9000 vehicles. The then American Ford Chairman, Ernest Breech, stated bluntly that the Wolfsburg factory was 'not worth a damn'.

Over 20 years later, Volkswagen is number one in Europe with 1,621,147 vehicles being produced during 1970 in its German plants alone. Every 8 seconds a new VW rolls off the production lines in Germany. During 1971, 70,000 VWs were sold in this country contributing greatly to the foreign manufacturers' over 20 per cent share of motor car sales in our home market. The 'ugly, noisy compromise' has lasted 30 years with over 16 million Beetles having been sold in more than 140 countries, and 8 million other VWs.

The production figure in 1949 of 9000 vehicles has been converted into about 10,000 a day, and the employees have grown to 62,000 at the Wolfsburg plant and a total of 200,000 in Germany and in overseas subsidiaries. The range of the VW has been supplemented by 1600 saloons, 'Fastbacks' and 'Variants', the Kharmann-Ghia coupes and convertibles, the delivery vans, motor caravans and micro-buses and the 411 LE fuel injection luxury saloons and estates with their famous 'cigar box computer' and recently the water-cooled VW K70. The ubiquitous Beetle, being produced at the rate of 3000 a day in Wolfsburg, has now caught up Ford's Model T as the world's best selling car of all time, and sits pretty at the top of British and American import lists. Expensive capital equipment never lies unproductively idle and VW was able recently to finance a several billion mark investment programme from its own resources and then pay a 18.5 per cent dividend to the shareholders. This kind of track record makes any manufacturer jealous, but I am hoping this case study will not merely produce envy of VW, but hopefully a recipe for success that we can learn from.

Discussing this subject with many UK business men I am told that the VW rise to fortune is due to the industrious and submissive labour force. I find little evidence at Wolfsburg that VW rely on this criterion. There can be little doubt that the VW triumph owes much to the genius of its management which for 20 years was headed by Professor Heinz Nordhoff, and is now under the chairmanship of Doctor Rudolf Leiding. With 62,000 employees in one plant alone, VW management realised they were too big a concern for 'paternalism' to work, and this increase in numbers over a 20 year period has not only involved considerable investment but also brought with it numerous social problems. Management realised that if the main business objective of a universal best selling 'people's' car was to be achieved then the concept of VW organisation was twofold. It was made up of the socio-system of people and their organisation, and a technical system incorporating plant and equipment and, of course, the end product. Neither could be viewed in isolation; if the VW was to be successful the socio-technical systems were always to be complementary and supportive.

If VW were to become any real threat to car competitors it could never come from the 'noisy, ugly, compromise' but the way in which it was made. It had to be industrial efficiency, innovation and improvement that won at the end of a day, and this could only be achieved through the worker and his work.

The economic importance of industrial peace cannot be overstated. Disruption affecting car assembly is at the heart of the problem rather than cost. Ford Europe Chairman Stanley Gillen recently claimed that he got 25 per cent more productivity from his continental assembly lines than his British. But it is not 'hard' work that is missing, but as VW indicated 'effective' work. Industrial disputes are partly to blame, but the 11 per cent absenteeism figure that disorganises Halewood and the sharp daily fluctuations at Dagenham are two factors barely existent in VW life. The reason for this, according to both VW management and union, is that the interests of the firm and the interests of the employees seem visibly identical. There is no division between 'them' and 'us' — everyone has a vested interest in the VW success. The economic reasoning is as simple. VW's annual wage bill is Dm 2500 million. A single day's strike costs the company at least Dm 30 million, over 1 per cent of the total year's wages. Money spent to ensure that disruptions occur seldom, strikes never, are a sound commercial investment. And the same is true with involvement and communication. Time spent in ensuring that the shop floor is involved in decision making regarding workers and their work can only be profitable. The same is also the case with hours spent on the negotiation of a new wage agreement thereby ensuring that when the deal has gone through it has the genuine support of the people whose lives it will affect.

At this juncture, it is worth mentioning the system of communication that exists within the Wolfsburg plant and contributes to the industrial peace. More than two-thirds of all its workers, professional, technical, white collar and manual, are organised in one industrial union, the I.G. Metall, Germany's massive and monolithic metalworking union which, with 2.2 million members, is Germany's strongest and most militant union.

There are four full time officials of this union at the Wolfsburg plant dealing with all local matters. There are 1450 shop stewards at the plant known as Vertraunsleute (men of confidence), and this works out at approximately 1 shop steward representative to 20 shop floor employees and up to about 50 white collar workers. These 1450 shop stewards maintain a close relationship with the Works Council members of the Metal Workers' Union. In the case of blue collar workers, these 1450 stewards meet every 2 weeks in groups relevant to their respective production areas. Their meetings last an hour and a half in works time. Shop stewards representing white collar workers meet every 4 weeks, the meeting lasting 2 or 3 hours in works time. At these meetings, the shop stewards report on topics and discuss various proposals ranging from pay and conditions, to training and education of all employees and production processes. Heading these meetings are the respective members of the Works Council known as the Betriebsrat which is a legally based body set up under the provisions of Federal law. The Works Council is elected by all employees in the factory and it is responsible to the whole working force which has elected it. It is not responsible to the union although there is provision for representation of the shop stewards on the Works Council to ensure harmony between the union organisation and the Works Council.

A grievance procedure would be something like this. Although there is a formal briefing meeting between the shop steward and his group, group meetings are normally considered by management to be an informal affair, for the group all work together. If one of the 20 on the shop floor has a problem he can take it to his union representative without waiting for the formal meeting to take place. The shop steward then discusses the particular grievance with the line management concerned *direct*. If he cannot obtain a satisfactory solution the Works Council acts as the lawyer, and a Works Council representative takes over the role of employee defence lawyer. Similarly, the Works Council representative may feel the employee and/or shop steward do not have a case although I am informed this happens very seldom. It is equally rare for a Works Council member to be approached to act as lawyer, since normally the shop steward can cope adequately with an employee grievance direct with management.

The controlling board of VW includes seven members elected by the firm's employees. These worker–directors are not just seven ciphers elected as a concession to industrial democracy and expected to sit silent while the 'real' managers take the 'real' decisions. Their influence on VW policy is as great as that of the other directors. In 25 years the Board has never gone against their recommendation on any issue affecting labour. Every 3 months a workers' meeting takes place during working hours at which the Works Council addresses the employees and problems of common interest are discussed. Invited by the Works Council, top management attends the meeting and the Chairman delivers a report on the situation of the company.

The briefing system is, therefore, that set out in Table 5.

In talking with a number of shop stewards it was apparent that one of the most important considerations was education and training. It was felt that education was 'absolutely essential for the shop stewards' for 'we are always negotiating with the management whether it be at union representative level or on the Betriebsrat'. All shop stewards may receive 2–4 weeks training per year which incorporates a variety of subjects from trade union legislation to economics, from human relations to effective speaking.

The main duties of the Betriebsrat are:

1 It has to discuss the problems of the workers at top management level.
2 It has to ensure the health and welfare of the employees.
3 It has to take the position of a lawyer and represent the employee if necessary, and attempt to find a solution to a specific problem if the 'local' shop steward has failed to solve a grievance.
4 It has to ensure equal pay for equal work or broadly similar work, and that wages and conditions are considered satisfactory.
5 It has to ensure the dignity of the worker has not been demeaned and at all times maintain the individuality and identity of each worker.

There are, of course, many other duties, but their Vice-President informed me that these five items were considered the most important. When one considers these items, and that the shop steward is responsible at local level as to their implementation and adherence, then it is clear why such emphasis is placed on the training requirements for such a responsible role. Speaking with a skilled toolmaker recently elected a shop steward, he told me that probably the main objectives of his role were similar to the French Revolution anthem of 'liberty, equality and fraternity'.

As I stated earlier, before discussing in further detail the communication process, the importance of industrial peace cannot be overstated. An encouragement for VW 'peace' must stem from their wage system. The opportunity to haggle over every individual job and draw unsettling comparisons with other workers' earnings often exacerbates

Table 5 The briefing system in the Volkswagen works.

Who meets who	When	For how long
Worker meets Betriebsrat	Whenever necessary	As long as required
Workers (works council)	Every 3 months	Anything from 3 hours 3 hours
Betriebsrat	Every 2 weeks	Anything from 1 hour to 3 hours
* Betriebsrat and the Vertraunsleute (men of confidence) of various production and office areas	Every 2 weeks	For 1½ hours
The shop stewards for the white collar side	Every month	For 2-3 hours approx.
The shop steward and his group of employees	Formally every 2 weeks but considered by management to be an informal briefing for the group works together	For ½ hour plus as necessary
The shop steward and his respective management	Any time	As long as necessary
Management and shop stewards	Every 3 months	As long as necessary

* Betriebsrat very rarely meets all 1450 shop stewards together (about once in every 6 months), for it is felt that as the Betriebsrat is a full time body coping with the work and conditions of 62,000 employees it can best serve them by meeting groups of shop stewards of various production units rather than by meeting all shop stewards en masse.

industrial unrest. The VW secret not only lies in the efficient communication set-up but also with the wages: not the size, but more the simplicity. With such an effective management to shop floor conversation and discussion system, it was not too difficult a task to implement a job evaluation scheme which offered seven grades for production workers and nine for skilled workers. Production workers are on a measured day work basis, that is the pace of work is one of the factors in the grading. Each grade is paid a flat hourly rate and the whole scheme is negotiated by the union and the management, policed by the shop stewards and generally supervised by a joint committee of the Works Council and management. The regional headquarters of I.G. Metall at Hanover negotiates central agreements with VW covering all their German factories. The productivity deal between the unions and the company for this year says that the production figure for the 'Beetle' must be 3000 a day. So the track is set at that speed and the most industrious worker is unable to exceed that target. As I indicated earlier, money and time spent on this kind of negotiation is a commercial investment. For, when the deal has gone through everyone is aware and confident that it has the genuine support of all those whose lives it will affect. And this type of negotiating procedure has ensured that VW has kept their efficient working lines running all year long, and that continuity of work has been guaranteed.

No pay system can be without its strains and injustices, but there is no question that the one in operation at VW has contributed to the success of the social side of the organisation. For, from the workers' point of view, it provides a high and stable income, as well as relaxing tensions between individuals and groups, and the tolerable work pace and organisation allows concentration and interest in the quality of work.

According to German industrial relations law, unions which encourage strikes before a wage agreement has run its full course can be prosecuted. Despite this German law, there have been recent 'illegal' strikes particularly in the coal and steel industries. VW management and unions feel that though the law may be wholly reasonable it is largely irrelevant. According to them, no power on earth can prevent workers from striking once tension and friction have begun to develop. The trick is to ensure that they are prevented from developing and if already present to diagnose the cause and prevent recurrence. The simplicity and fairness of the VW job evaluation and wages scheme has alleviated a possible source of employee discontent and tension.

Everyone in VW knows that the 'Beetle' is not the most powerful, beautiful or economical car in the world. But the company is selling quality and reliability. Producing quality and reliability is still a human problem for there are many jobs in car production which only human beings can do. But the price for a mass produced 'people's' car must never be unreliability, so what has been the answer at VW to the means of reducing the sources of unreliability? A communication process involving the worker and a wage system allowing a tension-free atmosphere and tolerable work pace have undoubtedly been powerful levers in enforcing VW high standards of workmanship. However, unanimous support is given to the contention that once the employee is interested in his work a large part of the problem of unreliability disappears.

The 'Beetle' has survived 25 years of detailed improvements with its original toughness and simplicity still heading its virtues. There have been about 3000 modifications to the original model that was designed by Ferdinand Porsche in the thirties. In fact, each of its 5000 parts has been changed in some way. Achieving both economies of scale and advantages of innovation in the same model is not unique to VW. British Leyland can claim as much for the Minor and the Mini. But VW has one important advantage in that 90 per cent of its total production enjoys these twin benefits. And much of the genius of innovation has come from its workers on the production line. In addition, the company grants premiums for suggestions for improvements received from the employees at rates negotiated between the Works Council and the factory management. These awards range up to DM 100,000. Some of the changes stemmed often from the briefing groups with the workers the shop stewards and management. It is law in Germany for management to tell the Works Council of any changes affecting the conditions of work, from shift times to holidays from remuneration to further education. No alteration can be made in the production process affecting the worker direct or automation be considered, without the comments and approval of the work force through its elected representatives on the Works Council.

The advantages of this system are many, perhaps the most important being the involvement of the workers in the job itself. As many as one third of the labour force own a VW and therefore they are customers as well as producers of the car, this giving them two reasons for also being VW's severest critics. And management allow them the opportunity to exercise their judgement and criticism of the product they are making. Coupled with this each employee is solely held responsible for the quality of his particular part of the end product. The responsibility is on his shoulders, and he is held accountable for the job he does. A job badly done will not only reflect on the individual but on his group. For in VW there are no individual piece workers; everyone is part of a group, and the leader of that group can be an elected man of confidence, namely the shop steward. All union matters concerning the group are handled by that shop steward. Supervisors are first line managers responsible in many instances for a number of the groups.

There is very little component work undertaken by a human being, for VW feel that giving a person a boring, routine job to do accentuates the risk of unreliability. For a person not interested in his task and not involved with his work load can only deteriorate in his performance, and that is something the company cannot afford. As many of the boring and routine jobs in car assembly as possible have been automated within VW. Automatic machinery with built-in sensors check errors and the quality control built into the production process minimises errors and unreliability. The jobs which only human beings can do have been studied to ensure that they are tasks which an individual will find satisfying and become involved in. Individuals and their groups are in the majority employed on sub-assembly work responsible for producing, for example, a *complete* transmission rather than a *part* of one. The genuine responsibility for this sub-assembly comes in a number of forms. A group on any part of the VW assembly line can:

1 Requisition their own materials and equipment without verification from a supervisor.
2 Have their individual budget for these materials and services which are seen to be complied with at the fortnightly briefing group sessions.
3 Have the authority to discard inferior quality material or sub-assembly work.
4 Have involvement at the briefing sessions for decisions affecting the sub-assembly and can organise their own working schedules and priorities knowing what the output target is. (This having been agreed during the wage negotiations for each job evaluated grade.)
5 Can initiate their own investigatory work, for instance a subjective decision regarding the engine or gearbox noise can be taken by the group in consultation with the supervisor and/or the inspector. The group (through the shop steward) can approach the service functions of inspector or manager direct.

It is considered by VW that this involvement of accountability for the employees has contributed to the successful reliability of the end product. It is not enough simply to 'remind' people of their responsibility, in this instance particularly for quality, but they must be held accountable and have this pressure on them if there is ever to be a noticeable decline in the percentage of defective articles. Having the responsibility for discarding inferior quality material and for rejecting defective components also allows them to correct the fault to prevent a future occurrence. Often inspectors in car assembly are too far removed from the production point of error to be in a position to correct a defect at source.

The self-supervising teams certainly allow the supervisors to carry out the important administrative functions as well as arranging for the long term needs of the production areas. The education and training role of the supervisor takes a lot of his time, for he has to ensure that the skill of the individuals in the groups is diverse enough to cope with sub-assembly as opposed to mere component production. Whenever jobs are automated under German law any worker displaced through the automation is entitled to be retained and retrained at company expense without any drop in pay. Many of the unskilled Italians that I spoke to were undergoing on-the-job craft training to enable them to join the groups on the assembly line. Similarly, the education for not only the Italians but other foreign workers, which includes Tunisians in large numbers, is extended into language laboratory classes in company time in order that they may learn German. With such a high percentage of foreign workers on the production line it is even more important that the groups are highly skilled and flexible to allow members of the team to have time off for retraining, craft appreciation, language classes and, of course, the exhaustive training schedule of the shop steward. A number of the supervisors and, in some areas of production, operators, were attending training classes offering the rudiments of data processing. With much of the boring, routine work being automated and computerised, it was felt that an appreciation of up to date technology would encourage people to understand and accept the sophistication of the capital intensive equipment.

Performance appraisal is another time consuming activity of the supervisor. It is extremely important that the groups have feedback on their performance. What is expected of them? How many parts? By what date? How many competent people have gone through that group? This case study represents another example of the necessity of feedback. As other studies will endorse, working blind, without comments of good or bad, is destructive.

The work itself has been made more complete. Opportunities are given whenever possible for demonstrable achievement by the groups and for their skills to be extended and for talents to be born. Individuals within the groups, including the leader, have a chance to develop competence and expertise, and possibilities for promotion and more challenging tasks are apparent. This may be the unskilled Italian learning the tricks of a toolmaker or the once-upon-a-time unskilled Tunisian having been elected a man of confidence and attending classes in effective speaking.

It is interesting to note that inspectors at VW get no extra pay. It is a position of status and an increase in reponsibility that certain individuals in groups take on when they have become 'known' experts, in judging certain portions of the production process, for example, cracks in chrome work. Any verification of inspection methods from outside the group, for instance an inspector checking keys which have been checked once before by the production group, is bound to increase costs, and in return may only give a small improvement in overall reliability. All the more reason for placing accountability for quality and reliability on the shoulders of the person actually doing the job. Once the worker is interested, involved and responsible he can be trusted to do it efficiently as has proved the case in VW. It doesn't even have to have a price tag as is the case with the VW inspector. Given the opportunity to develop he either responds or he does not. If he does, then it is part of the job. We see in other studies examples of individuals being presented with opportunity for achievement and self-development. Things don't get worse, for people either accept the opportunity and achieve something or they do not.

I mentioned earlier in the book that absence of motivation brought not complaint, but apathy, laziness, friction, etc. Absence of good working conditions will bring annoyance and complaint. An example of this can be taken from VW. The employees will complain about the fringe benefits of anything from profit sharing to death grants, from canteens to working hours. And one of the main duties of the Betriebsrat as indicated earlier was to maintain a satisfactory standard for all these benefits, and more. But they do not have apathy, unrest, laziness or friction on a scale that is often experienced in other manufacturing concerns which, too, have plied their workers with all the carrots.

The problem is diagnosed another way. People do not just work for bread alone, but how can they complain about something they have never received. If all they are given is bread then when they are apathetic and dissatisfied that is all they will ask for in an attempt to alleviate that dissatisfaction. VW realise that individuals have more to their make-up than the need for bread. They have dignity and share desires for success and self-respect. They need to be involved and have a say in things. This is all part of the VW policy, the social side of their socio-technical system. As other car manufacturers have found out to their cost, so much seems to depend on the labour situation. One just cannot treat the individual on the assembly line as a mere component in a production process.

VW have learned from experience that some people will respond to opportunities for self-respect and self-development or they will not. Some individuals seize the opportunities much more readily than others. Whatever the result, it is a private experience between that individual and his job. It will not bring complaint and the social side of the company policy has ensured that apathy and laziness, absenteeism and unreliability, tension and friction have been kept to a minimum and certainly have seldom been causes for disruption and, hopefully, will remain so.

We cannot transplant the whole set of social and economic circumstances of Western Germany since the war in which VW arose. Nor in one sense should one wish to, for the firm is the economic bastion living in the shadow of the borderland between east and west. However, as mentioned earlier in the study, part of the VW doctrine was that if it were to become any real threat to car competitors it could never come from the 'noisy, ugly compromise' but the way in which it was made. Of course, VW claim special features of design and construction from the solid chassis which gives the Beetle extra strength and durability to the 'dipped' paint work lasting longer. But the company are aware that UK pacemakers from the Cortina to the Mini and through a whole range of sports models can offer alternative attractions. That is why the way in which VWs are made becomes so important.

VW claim they can secure 1 in 20 of Britain's motor car sales long before 1975; all that is stopping them at the moment is the tariff barriers which separate Europe from the UK. All that will change, of course, should Britain join the Common Market. For British cars, too, offer tremendous opportunities for selling in the huge Continental market when costs are no higher than Fiat and Renault. But the British car industry's home sales will no longer be protected. And VW can guarantee an effective production line that never stops running except some weekends and at night. The reasons for this I have reiterated in the study.

They have given their workers the opportunity and the chance to contribute to an industrial life of which they are capable. This was why the leading United States engineering societies presented an award to the employees of Volkswagen in Germany as well as to Heinz Nordhoff and posthumously to Porsche, for 'The development of the VW, which in concept, engineering, design and production has made available to the world an automobile of small size for multiple uses with unique attributes of universality'.

If we can learn from this, who would ask it otherwise?

case study nine

The Volvo Group

The Volvo Group of Companies has quite a significance for the Swedish community apart from the fact that it is Sweden's largest manufacturer of transport products. The company is the country's largest taxpayer: is responsible for 8 per cent of all Swedish exports: employs 41,000 as a work force within her plants, plus a dealer network providing jobs for 10,000. A further 15,000 jobs are provided through the sub-contractors. Two per cent of the country's population derives its income from Volvo.

Exports account for 75 per cent of Volvo's total production and her products are sold on 120 markets. Perhaps better known for its car production, the range of products extends through buses, trucks, marine and industrial engines, to construction farm and forestry machinery, aircraft engines and a components line production for armoured vehicles.

Pehr Gyllenhammar, at 37 and the head of the Volvo Group world-wide, is considered Sweden's 'Trudeau' and many see him as a possible future Prime Minister. The Social Democrats (Labour party' which have been in power for 40 years face perhaps their most crucial election in September 1973. It is at this election that Pehr Gyllenhammar may make his entry into politics. I was never able to ascertain his political standpoint, but it varied between the Liberal Folkparti or the Moderate Unionist party depending on whom I spoke to! Certainly some of the characteristics which he portrays can also be found within Volvo's Head Office in Gothenburg—dynamic, efficient, good looking, with an air of wealth.

The Swedish system of industrial relations has long been widely recognised as one of the most harmonious and stable in the world and this is reflected within Volvo, with only a one day strike recorded in the history of the company. Therefore industrial disruption through labour strikes and disputes is not a problem within the Volvo company or within Sweden, although there are signs on the horizon.

The peaceful scene is beginning to be spoilt by activist groups and, although the Swedes are not eager to acknowledge the fact, there have been an increasing number of wildcat strikes, sit downs, slow downs and the like—many of which have never come to the knowledge of the public.

However, the threat of industrial action is still a weapon seldom used compared with the record in our own country. What is a problem within Sweden, and is highlighted in the plants of its highest taxpayer, is the high cost of labour. Within Volvo the costs of maintaining the work force are increased dramatically when one considers that the company needs to have about a seventh of their total work force in reserve because of absenteeism and labour turnover.

There is a chronic shortage of Swedes willing to work on production and assembly line work. The reason is not difficult to discover—they spend more per capita on education than any other country in the world. To an educated work force the word 'factory' means boring and monotonous work, it means noise and dirt, accident risks, hazardous substances, cramped positions. This has been endorsed over the years by the public debates resulting in various 'laws' regarding work conditions and the physiological adjustment to work has long been the domain of the personnel departments.

An educated work force is setting its sights higher than ever before when choosing its occupation. Industry is not therefore the first choice for a recruit and a lot of 'jelly beans' have to be offered to attract the labour force necessary to prevent production being disrupted. Sweden, like the UK, has an unemployment problem, yet to obtain employees for production line work it has to set its sights further than within its own boundaries. 50 per cent of the Volvo production force is immigrant labour—from Finland, Yugoslavia, Greece, and other countries. These workers build their own communities outside and inside the work place, forcing communications to be distributed in four languages (in some instances more) and placing a strain on the country's social system which is becoming more evident each year.

When no other work is available man resorts to his need to survive and with the graduate community in Sweden this has meant the realisation that a degree doesn't necessarily mean a passport to a professional or white-collar position. It has meant that increasingly more and more graduates commence their work life on the shop floor— and although I am convinced through my own experience that they will benefit from this in later life—in the initial stages, in mass, they bring a great deal of concern and confusion to their employers. They do not tolerate the boring, straight-jacketed jobs of production work. They demand change. They form their own activist groups within the companies, forcing either management or unions to concede changes within the working environment. As these groups get more powerful, as they will within the next few years in this country and as they are already in Sweden, the unions try to cooperate with their demands in an effort to ensure that the 'illegal' movement does not become a threat to the legal organisations.

Another threat to the company is the high absenteeism and labour turnover, and recent studies within the Volvo group discovered that dissatisfaction with the job itself was encouraging people to leave the industry or to participate in late timekeeping, Mondays-off, skiving or extended absence certificates when the common cold was the simple diagnosis. These symptoms are familiar to us in this country (perhaps with a little more bloody-mindedness than among the well-mannered Scandinavians). But perhaps no company has involved itself more actively in a programme of job enrichment, built on the foundations of across-the-board training and re-organisation, as those in Sweden and, in particular, the Volvo Group of Companies.

In the introduction to this article Pehr Gyllenhammar indicated that he did not look upon these problems as a 'threat'. As he told his shareholders at the last annual general meeting.

'Our ability to recruit employees and lower labour turnover and absenteeism will affect our competitive ability in the future.'

That could be something to be reckoned with, for despite its being a tiddler in the world scene of car producers Volvo can still manage to laugh at Renault and Fiat losing money (to name but two). It can smile as it manages a 10·3 per cent profit margin for the last year and record profits, as the company has its debut on the London Stock Market, are a 43 per cent increase over last year at £60 million.

In addition it is doubling its EEC assembly plant in Belgium, expanding to 100,000 cars and £20 million in the process. It is also building a one-million-a-year car engine plant in France with Renault and Peugeot and has negotiated a third stake in Dutch DAF. Add to this the £20 million that was spent on a new development and testing lab, allwoing Volvo to be well ahead with its safety features and anti-pollution standards for the US market, where it is already second in the imported car sales listings. Apart from spending between 5 and 10 per cent of its gross sales revenue on research, development and tooling, the company is building a new assembly plant at Kalmar in Sweden at a cost of £10 million. The important point is that this is already considered to be costing 10 per cent more than the developing of a comparable conventional assembly plant as Volvo attempt to find the cure for the production line disease of dying people.

Change was necessary therefore to reduce the 46 per cent labour turnover figure in the Volvo plants in Gothenburg alone. It was necessary to reduce the absenteeism, bloody-mindedness and human error which often accompanies a task which is boring and monotonous. It was necessary to correct the problems of the massive disruption that can occur when the sensitive production line is attacked by the interference of late time-keeping and absence of people and parts.

Change was necessary to make factory work fashionable. As the company President said:

'With the present educational system we have people who demand more of their jobs – they won't in my opinion, in the long run, put up with simple or monotonous jobs. They would like to see "richer" jobs and longer job cycles.'

Thus there were two initiatives for change within the Volvo company. One came from a group of employees themselves suggesting to their respective management or union representatives that they would 'like to swop jobs now and again to break the tedium'. The second initiative came from the senior group management, most noticeably the President, mainly due to the economic reasons mentioned earlier.

Before I look further at the company philosophy, let's look at the first attempt at work restructuring. This originated from the employees themselves and is now an accepted working order of the upholstery department.

The upholstery shop in the car palnt at Gothenburg was riddled with high labour turnover and absenteeism mainly due to the women, who were employed there, needing days off or even a complete change of job owing to the back-breaking tasks necessary in putting a car seat together. Each woman did a different job extending through a range of chores (attaching the back rest to the seat, mounting fittings, positioning headrests). The women in the department suggested a system of rotation where the girls changed their jobs daily, even taking it in turns to act as group supervisor and quality inspector. The plate 1 shows the women in the workshop and the arrows indicate the order in which the women change their jobs every day.

The advantages of the system are many, flexibility being the most important. Before, when an employee went absent the production was badly disrupted or might not start for half an hour until a replacement was found. Now, when a new addition joins the team, all the group can help in teaching the recruit the ropes as all are familiar with the various routines. The turnover in this group is now very low (under 10 per cent compared with a figure over 40 per cent a couple of years ago). It has been decided to extend the system of work groups and job rotation to

Plate I   Job rotation in the upholstery shop at Volvo.

other employees within Volvo. Management support is vital for wide-scale programmes of this nature.

Motivation cannot cure technical incompetence and the basic feature of any job enrichment programme is training. As Pehr Gyllenhammar put it:

> 'Job enrichment depends very much on how well trained the work force are, on how well they will respond to the type of responsibility they are being given and it takes – and this is very important – it takes very strong leadership. True leadership in my opinion is to give responsibility and to have trust in people.'

Therefore a new organisational structure was evolved with the basic principle of the organisation and of the group being that of decentralised responsibility. Each product line and marketing unit forms a profit centre. In order to train and select the personnel needed to support new jobs or undertake them Volvo has a regular staff training scheme plus an executive training programme.

Induction and training of new recruits last at least 130 hours and consist of information about the work conditions (eg safety), and practical work in the training workshops and shop floor. These training hours are spread out over three periods during the employee's first 16 weeks within the company. After six months the employee can be considered for further development.

I discovered when within Volkswagen in Germany that group working bore its greatest advantage in allowing personnel to be freed for long periods of time for training purposes, whether this was in language classes for the new immigrant labour or in leadership classes for potential group leaders and foremen. The system works just as well in Sweden with a different labour force and a different society. With our own entry into the EEC and a freer movement of labour, training classes, most probably in English, will become the rule rather than the exception. It would be sad if this new age of Europeans were denied the opportunity for growth and development because the system did not allow it.

The modern leadership requirement referred to by the Volvo President is achieved through continuous education in communication techniques, economics, staff welfare and group behaviour. It has long been realised that a group's function depends on the extent to which its leader succeeds in stimulating it and engaging it to carry out its task. The systematic programme of leader development is an important part of the programme for the foremen and group leaders. Volvo is no exception among companies using modern behavioural programmes in discovering that the hardest people to convince of the authenticity of job enrichment are the first liners, eg foremen. In suggesting to them that they should delegate the chores of their jobs, eg red tape and checking, to the person actually carrying out the function, one suggests that the transfer of supervision to the operator can be equated with the redundancy of the supervisor.

Ingvar Barrby is the foremen in the upholstery shop at the Gothenburg plant and his job has been radically changed through the work structuring programme. He used to be laden with the chores of checking and disciplining a group of individual women on assembly work. Many who have shared this task can sympathise. Some of the women were not turning up for work due to the children, illness, or simply not being bothered. Shifts would bring the absence of individuals or parts that would disrupt the schedules. Unless he spent a great deal of his time checking and supervising the work being carried out by each individual, mistakes would occur and the responsibility for error would lie on the shoulders of the foreman. Not being involved with their job, there was no commitment by these women to ensure the quality of the product. Today his job has become more of a sociologist than a checker. He has entered the people business—he is responsible for selecting people for his group, ensuring that they are trained to do all the varigus tasks. He has become responsible for their development and growth. He has become a leader of a group of now closely-knit individuals who are aware they are working together as a team, aware whom they are letting down if they don't come to work. He is motivated by having his own talents of experience with the company over a great many years shared and stretched. He is encouraged by looking after and developing a team of motivated individuals as opposed to supervising robots. They are motivated by being fully responsible for their own work, carrying the can should errors occur and reaping the satisfaction of seeing their group produce an end product.

In another part of the plant line 1·3 labour turnover and absenteeism have been reduced by similar amounts. In plate 2 the arrows indicate the exchange of jobs that occur every fourth hour on the assembly line. Here the work concerns rear bumpers, instrument dashboard work inside the car, mounting of door locks, grill console, brake pipe units. Further along this line another group change their jobs every day with a weekly job sheet looking like this:

Monday	assembly of petrol pump
Tuesday	assembly of side windows
Wednesday	assembly inside the car
Thursday	assembly on rear end of car
Friday	new schedules

In other parts of the plant the production flow may not allow this sort of method and in this instance the fitter often follows a body along the line and works on the same body for up to an hour.

119

Plate 2   Job rotation on the assembly line at Volvo.

Employees have been taken off straight and conventional assembly into group assembly for a while before returning to their original tasks. They have always preferred the new system saying that they experience an increased sense of fellowship with their colleagues as they 'get experience of each other's work'. They enjoy the wider scope of their new jobs.

As was discovered in Volkswagen, when they changed to this type of production one of the gains was also that of quality. The groups have the responsibility themselves to discard inferior quality material and the fault can be corrected at source. Volvo have gone further, they have supported their teams with group leaders and foremen familiar with the theories of the behavioural sciences and human development. They have been taught that it is simply not enough to remind people that they are responsible: they must be held *accountable*.

Volvo have implemented a joint consultative procedure where the group and their foreman can discuss all technical and environmental matters relating to the group, company, or individuals. Quality control can be discussed at line level instead of becoming a topic for chit-chat further up the hierarchy.

1500 employees within Volvo are now involved in the work structuring programmes. There is certainly a difference in walking round a production unit full of enthusiastic and alive groups from a trip through the graveyard that conventional assembly lines often deteriorates into. There is no doubt in my mind that work is more efficient when it is enjoyable, and genuine motivation within a company is the pay-off from the *two-way* participation possible through job enrichment.

Volvo estimate that in the initial introduction to change only 15 per cent of the employees concerned are immediately in favour of cooperating. About 30 per cent couldn't care less one way or the other and the remainder have to be won over. This is where the training programme comes in. Supervisors and foremen already equipped as trainers explain to the employees the need for change and train them to cope with it. The employees have however a further support from the trade unions.

In the Gothenburg area alone Volvo have 14,645 employees of which 9383 are production workers belonging to the one union of metal workers. This figure means that 98 per cent of all shop floor employees are in the one union. In the white collar union (Tjanstemannens Centralorganisation = TCO = Central Organisation of Salaried Employees) 78 per cent of their administrative staff of 4762 and all the 500 foremen can rely on union support.

Stig Edin is a Huvudskyddsombud in Svenska Metall/arbetareforbundet a member of the local board of Sweden's largest and most monolithic structure, the Union of Metal Workers. His knowledge of the Swedish trade union movement was only surpassed by his knowledge of our own and certain points he made a ring of truth about them:

'Perhaps the biggest difference as we understand it between industrial relations in Great Britain and in Sweden is that your unions are afraid of change – whilst we have learned to participate and accept rationalisation and change through training.'

Management and labour in Sweden as in UK confront each other as two strongly organised forces—a stable balance of power. Certainly they meet in Sweden with an unusual degree of mutual confidence, more than I have encountered in any other country. This confidence spreads through the negotiating of their differences to creating joint machinery for peace on the labour market and security in areas of common interest. The two major organisations involved are Svenska Arbetsgivareforeningen (SAF) which is the Swedish Employers' Federation, with 24,000 members employing 1,350,000 persons and Landsorganisationen (LO) which is the Swedish TUC with 1,650,000 members including more than 90 per cent of all blue collar workers. One of the first agreements made, to create mutual respect between industry and labour, set forth the employers' right to run business affairs as they saw fit and recognised the workers' right to organise. Thus closed shops are very rare. Member federations and firms within SAF are not allowed to sign any contracts making union membership a requisite of employment—but no employer can use his freedom to hire non-union labour as a weapon to weaken the trade union movement. There also exists a Labour Market Council which is a special arbitrating body jointly set up by SAF and LO which deals with such conflicts as unfair dismissals, discriminations and disputes. At all levels the prime interest managment and labour organisations have in common is to keep all negotiations unhampered by Government regulation.

Collective bargaining agreements are made at this level for all industries and form the current base for peace in Swedish industry. They are known as Saltsjobaden agreements, after the town outside Stockholm which has become the traditional meeting place for the top labour-management organisations. However, the members of the LO are sovereigns in their own right, and are free to arrange their own wage agreements and, of course, can call a strike if they wish. But if a union initiates a strike which involves more than three per cent of its membership it forfeits a right to financial assistance from LO during the conflict. As the LO is usually represented at all important member wage negotiations, it is very seldom that strike action is considered necessary or that the LO would sanction such an action.

However, in the public sector collective bargaining works far from smoothly; there have been two major conflicts since 1966 which involved Government intervention. It was ironic that these disruptions should have occurred in the highest paid industries and were concerned with job conditions and environmental issues and *not* with wage agreements. The most militant disputes in this country originate in those unions and industries where the basic wage is higher than most. It was following these disputes that the SAF/LO and the Labour Market Council turned their attention to the ways in which people were *used* in industry as well as how they were *treated*.

In all my encounters in Sweden, whether within LO, or at SAF, with my colleagues in EF (Ekonomisk Foretagsledning), or in the various companies like SAAB-SCANIA or the Swedish State Power Board, the same point came over and over again and it can best be summarised by Pehr Gyllenhammar:

'The Unions in Sweden have put a lot of money into education and training for their own members – they are well trained in management and understand management problems and this helps us to negotiate with them.'

Wherever initiative for change originates, from the work group itself, from the President of the company or from middle management, it has the support of information and consultancy advisory services from the Labour Market Council and SAF. SAF's technical department boss, Anders Noren, runs a department specifically engineered to advise on the problems and support necessary for wide scale rationalisation of the sort being carried out in Volvo. The individual's reaction to his work, his opportunities for feeling motivated and stimulated by what he does and his participation in deciding matters that affect his own work have come into the forefront of debate, and have influenced the activities of the labour-management organisations. With all the top organisations so immersed in the benefits to be reaped from job enrichment, it is understandable that their influence has spread to many firms within Sweden apart from Volvo. Some have started experiments in partnership with these organisations that amount to highly ambitious pilot programmes involving teams of behavioural scientists. Other firms (and there are many) have set more modest sights and are exploring new paths perhaps not as radical as Volvo's and I have mentioned briefly SAAB-SCANIA's work later in the book.

We are seeing ourselves the price we pay for not wishing to change and entry into the EEC will provide us with more glimpses. The wish to participate more in our working life is being heard from all sides of society, even from our prisons. Maybe we can even learn from Sweden, where experiments in Tillberga Prison near Vaesteraas allow prisoners a greater say in running their lives. The prisoners work a 40-hour week with little opportunity for the boredom which breeds militancy. For a 40-hour week they get market rates for equivalent jobs being done outside, allowing them to earn up to £130 per month. With this money a prisoner can pay back fines and compensation to the victims of their crime, and send money home to his wife and children. It is a far cry from earnings of our prisoners between 65p and £1.50 a week.

Almost certainly the biggest test for the UK is going to be in its ability to *cope* with *change*.

Pehr Gyllenhammar again:

'it should be possible to arrive at satisfactory solutions on those points where mutual accusations of business, labour and Government can be replaced by constructive discussions,'*

The author is grateful to many people within Sweden who have contributed to her work and hospitality. In particular Pehr Gyllenhammar President of the Volvo Group and the following members of his staff in Gothenburg:

Lars Ahren and Hans Blenner, Karl Maniette, Berth Jonsson and Sigvard Hoggren. Both the upholstery shop foreman—Ingvar Barrby and the shop steward Stig Edin were particularly helpful. Other people were of valuable assistance in particular, Anders Noren of the Swedish Employers Federation, and Lars-Olaf Odengran and colleagues at EF (Ekonomisk Foretagsledning) in Stockholm.

I have also included in this study some activities within the SAAB-SCANIA Group and I would like to thank both Goran Sandberg and

Sven Yngwe for their help and Kaj Holmelius of Production Engineering for his valuable assistance.

Finally I would like to thank Bo Widergren of the Swedish State Power Board for **just** managing to get me to my 'plane on time.

brief examples

It is interesting to note one of the large scale changes in the **Jensen Motor Company** a few years ago when it was fighting for survival involved the number of inspectors being reduced to zero. This was to impress on the men themselves that the quality of the product arose from their own integrity and nobody else's responsibility. Making redundant superfluous supervision in its old sense of the word has certainly improved the quantity and quality of the Jensen product. Again, any changes like this one had to have an ally in the union. The Managing Director at that time, Carl Duerr, told the unions that the company were not producing the right quantity and quality of a car and that twice as many cars per persons were needed if the company were to survive. The unions were asked: 'If this is not viable tell me so; if it is, help me to do it'.

The Jensen Interceptor on the market today has certainly proved that things have gone in the right direction with this company and the 1967 loss of £82,000 has turned by 1971 into a comfortable profit. Perhaps teaching the shop stewards how to read a profit and loss account as part of their training curriculum has played a part in the success of the Jensen product.

Finally, we have seen in many of the studies the importance of working within groups towards a final and shared objective. Two other fields where I have encountered this group involvement accompanying an improved motivating task is in the field of dry cleaning and laundry and also in the precision aircraft industry.

Many of the jobs in laundry work are not only boring and routine, but very little pleasure is derived from them at all. **Watford Launderers and Cleaners** have solved many of their problems of dull work by

Anthony Clark Partners Ltd., Sevenoaks

Figure 9   How three employees of Watford Launderers and Cleaners have been recognised.

placing individuals into group activity. Figure 9 will indicate how that company has not only given recognition and identity to these girls, in this instance Ada, Theresa and Margaret, but made them accountable to the customer direct for the quality of the product.

Apart from resulting in improved quality of end product and a decrease in labour turnover, the direct contact between launderer and client has resulted in these individuals at the most feeling more committed and responsible for their work and at the least receiving Christmas chocolate boxes from happy customers!

The other encounter is in the field of dry cleaning, in the **Hills of Fife Unit Dry Cleaning Shops.**

There are two types of Dry Cleaning Shops

   Receiving Shops: Work sent to the factory.
   Unit Shops: Work done on the premises.

Not for bread alone

The Unit Shop: usual organisation

1 man (manager) operates the dry cleaning machine, spotting and pressing.

1 woman on the counter (manageress).

1 woman helping on the counter, or helping with spotting and pressing.

The Hills group found advantages with a Team, formed in Unit Shops as follows:

4 girls all on the same pay, made up of a basic wage plus commission.

(2 girls' wages = 1 manager's wage on 'usual organisation'.)

They are able to cover for each other.

Any 3 are able to run the shop and give a 1 hour service. The only prescription laid down by the company:

The hours the shop is to be open.

That it must give the 1 hour service if required.

Within reason, subject to this prescription, the girls work mutually convenient hours. When very busy, some will start early in the morning. When quiet, they can take time off to do shopping and get their hair done, etc. The outstanding thing is that the team is committed to doing the job.

The quality is very good, and production is way beyond anything possible in even the best run factory. The press is the limiting factor. The turnover achieved in some of these shops is more than double the work which could be got through one press in a factory.

The woman on the counter changes from colluding with the customer against the factory, to feeling that she is representing the operatives who are going to do the work. The unit team system is almost as big a change again: the person accepting the work is one of the team which is going to process it. In turn, the team has a commitment to do that work which it has accepted.

Payment

All 4 girls receive the same pay. This is made up of a basic amount which is paid regardless of sales. Above a certain sales figure, commission is paid on a sliding scale. This sliding scale is the reverse of the type normally used in incentive schemes, in that the rate of commission increases at the higher rate of sales. This is, of course, a situation where this can be done confidently in that the unit shops are capital intensive with a high break even point, but above that a good profit margin.

Not for bread alone

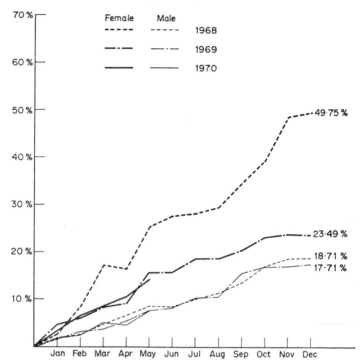

Figure 10   How employed labour turnover was reduced in the Hellermann Deutsch company.

As will be seen from Figure 10 the female labour turnover figure at **Hellermann Deutsch,** a member of the **Bowthorpe Group,** has been markedly reduced from 49·75 per cent in 1968 to a cumulative 22 per cent in late 1971. This company produces a range of high reliability electrical electronic components with a large percentage of the 8000 different component styles which come within the range falling into a 'lifeline' category.

The high precision components require a high level of individual operator integrity in manufacture and above average levels of operator concentration on job content. Here again, work patterns are structured into units with a supervisor to every 10 – 12 girls. A communication structure is used to develop the girls' sense of identity with the company's efforts in this market place, identifying to them needs for accuracy, concentration and integrity. The continuous communication gives a two way input to management on questions of environment, job distribution and job content.

128

A part of the communications link is the ideas scheme which produces a high level of job content improvements under guarantee of evaluation by the Board within 7 days. There is a 4 monthly salary review in operation which encompasses in depth review of efficiency, aptitude and all operation work on a flat rate payment system.

The girls are taught and encouraged to be job flexible, their skills extended in order that the company can compete in industries where speed and change are vital factors. Competition to enter the 'flying squad,' the mobile assembly group, is strong and the team is made up of the most competent and versatile of the unit team girls. There is a high accountability for self-supervision in the structure of each job and the depth of involvement of the job and its implications have contributed with careful selection of operators to a decrease in costly turnover figures.

This provides us with another example of a once-upon-a-time component in the production process being treated as an individual. An individual with hopes and aspirations, skills and latent talents, having them realised through the involvement and participation that is possible with job enrichment.

The SAAB-SCANIA Group is third largest in Sweden in terms of turnover (amounting to approximately £411 million). The total number of employees is approximately about 30,000. Its range of products extends from cars, trucks, buses, engines to computers and electronics, components from needle valves to fittings for ships and nuclear power plants. This organisation, too, is immersed in job enrichment programmes and like Volvo has discovered that training is one of the most important of all issues. Training is required so that every employee is capable of understanding not only how the company works but also the importance of his own individual work effort. A training course package for all employees is:

economics : so that the relationship between personnel work effort and the company's total costs can be understood

product knowledge : so that the importance of the individual work effort to the task and its function within the finished product can be understood

technology : completely adapted to the employee's work involving subjects such as the design of machines, maintenance, measurement techniques, quality control.

This package grows as the employee grows through the organisation and involves the human relationship and leadership training that was also undertaken within Volvo. In the SAAB-SCANIA gasoline engine plant individual assembly line work has been replaced by groups of girls working together. There are three fitters in each group.

Crankshafts, connecting rods and pistons, flywheels, manifolds and

Plate 3 Group working in the gasoline engine plant at SAAB-SCANIA.

complete cylinder heads (with valves and cam shafts) are fitted in this manner. Group assembly is arranged as six loops and plate 3 shows the assembled components being transported from one production group on a trolley to another group. After group assembly the engine is ready for testing and it is provided with the carburettor or the throttle housing for the electronic fuel injection, ignition distributor, camshaft chain and so on. The production schedule for these groups is set every ten days. The girls can therefore work daily, however they wish, as long as the targets are observed by the tenth day.

Group cohesion :

Once, on the conventional assembly line, the work cycle was 1.8 minutes. This has now been extended from a minimum of ten minutes to a maximum of 30 minutes when all the assembly is done and the girls see the entire engine through. The importance of a lengthened work cycle should not be under-rated. After sprains and strains, nervous disorders along with headache and debility are the most common cause of days lost from work within the UK. (page 14 NFBA). When the work cycle is lengthened the figures for absenteeism drop dramatically and this has certainly been the case also in Sweden where, as I mentioned earlier, absenteeism and resultant labour turnover have been considered as major reasons for implementing this type of programme.

As at Volvo, the new system of group assembly has several advantages. Flexibility again is foremost, in the event of a brief shortage of components, or illness of fitters, the group can be temporarily disbanded and a new group can be formed. In addition, should there be a flood of rush orders, then the number of groups can be increased accordingly. A better utilisation of the manpower resources is obtained. Small, autonomous, groups provide a realistic means of improving job satisfaction, but naturally it cannot be extended to embrace all systems within a mass production system. Group assembly requires a larger floor space than a conventional assembly line and this costs a great deal more money (ten per cent was indicated with the Volvo Kolmar plant). If group assembly were to be extended to the truck chassis workshop at SAAB-SCANIA for example the building would have to be twice as large as that currently in use. Production would then be uneconomical. We have to be efficient, but we also have to be human – too much 'humanisation' would equal inefficiency and probably anarchy, therefore a happy medium must be sought. Within SAAB-SCANIA their industrial engineers are continually searching for new methods and alternatives to group working for creating greater productivity and increased job satisfaction, where group assembly is neither practical nor feasible. The initiative for the SAAB-SCANIA experiments stem from the industrial engineering department and, as its head Palle Berggren said:

'these experiments may be regarded as only one phase in the development of enhanced industrial democracy.'

The Chairman of the local union branch of the Metal Workers Union, Arne Gustavsson, said that

'We have to work together so that we can jointly improve our working environment and natural collaboration between different employees must be established. This can be done if the groups have better training.'

It was considered that the new ideas could not operate within the UK because 'the unions would not allow it'. Perhaps industry and its management becomes complacent and although it may well not prove possible for assembly lines to be rearranged here as in Sweden, there must surely be greater scope for other forms of job enrichment. For example, greater voice in discussions relating to the work and its environment, individuals and/or groups requisitioning their own materials, further opportunities for on-the-job training. A greater scope for the delegation of foreman chores and checking duties. Thure Garbenius a foreman at SAAB-SCANIA and Chairman of the local branch of the Swedish Foreman's and Supervisors Association said:

'I believe that the role of the foreman has begun to change. We are being given greater responsibility, but responsibility emphasising planning and personnel management, areas which may have been neglected somewhat in the past. Since we are spared a lot of routine work which the groups themselves can take care of, we have more time to care for our personnel. Supervisor training will have to shift emphasis. Not every supervisor is inclined to view these developments with interest. Especially the older foremen who see them as intrusions into their special field. This is where training is important.'

What I felt was most important in all these companies doing more than any other to improve the job contents of their individuals, was their willingness to share their problems and mistakes. One problem admitted was that relating to foremen. The first line manager is perhaps the only genuine manager we have – he was promoted to that position from the shop floor and didn't gain it through his status or the colour of his school tie. They invariably are the most loyal people in a company, and changes of the type described here can be taken as a personal attack on their role. There is no denying that there is a great need for training for these employees. There is much to be done in the planning of work environments, corporate developments, and future growth of the employees. All of which should have been done to a greater·extent in the past but the manager who should have been occupied with these subjects was too busy doing things which could so easily have been done further down the hierarchy.

What is a chore for one man can often be a challenge for a subordinate, and as long as training is given to both individuals, then there is no reason why delegation should not pay off. As I said, motivation cannot cure incompetence and training is the basis for a programme of this nature. Communication and understanding are of paramount importance and this was emphasised particularly within Volvo who place great emphasis on the briefing session and face-to-face consultation between management/union/group leaders and selected individuals. It is doubtful whether without an effective exchange in these areas that a job enrichment programme could get off the ground, and be seen by the employees to be a genuine attempt at making the company more productive simultaneous with the standard of work life for its employees.

conclusion

Without comment, but with grateful thanks to the author and the publishers for their kind permission, I reproduce an extract from *The Territorial Imperative – A Personal Inquiry into the Animal Origins of Property and Nations* by Robert Ardrey (Collins, 1967).

'Let us remind ourselves: the planarian worm is an aquatic creature so primitive in the evolutionary scale that it lacks a true central nervous system, possesses a brain consisting of nothing but two enlarged ganglia connecting its two lateral nerves, lacks a stomach or rectum or anything resembling a modern digestive system, and while capable of laying an egg is equally capable of dividing itself in two and growing a new head on the front of its old rear section. Since it can grow that head in six days, we may safely assume that the planarian's brain is an organ of no great planarian concern. And we may also assume that had the planarian worm been a creature of natural invention at any time in the last half billion years, it would have incorporated into its old-fashioned architecture a modern gadget or two. It therefore seems likely that the creature is a left-over from those hazy pre-Cambrian days of evolving life about which we know so little. But when we say that, we talk of ages belonging to the same time scale as that which absorbs the cosmologist. When we look at the planarian we are looking back into the history of life, just as when we observe a quasar we are looking back into the history of all things.

Jay Boyd Best and his colleague Irvin Rubinstein began their Washington experiments with the planarian in 1958. Their initial interest was to discover just how much such an all-but-brainless being could be taught. Most learning-and-memory experiments with the planarian have had a weakness, that the learning has been a matter of inducing a conditional reflex, the all-purpose tool in the kit of most American psychologists. But this kind of learning, called "classical conditioning," is losing ground among our more advanced observers of behavior. What intrigued Best was that higher accommodation called "instrumental learning" by which, in pursuit of a desirable goal involving choice of actions, one learns to choose the right path and reject the wrong. A creature as simple as the planarian worm might conceivably be "taught" by electric shock a reflex to avoid this and accept that. But could this primitive being lacking sex, rectum, circulatory system, a modern nervous hook-up, a brain that could not be regrown in a few days, learn to choose between the rewarding and the unrewarding? And if so, what was he choosing with?

It took little effort for Best and Rubinstein to demonstrate that the worm could not only learn to choose, but could learn with dismaying aptitude. They constructed a plastic maze, a simple device with a Y-shaped channel connecting three wells. A worm would be placed in one well of the flooded maze, then the water would be drained out. Since the planarian cannot long survive in a dry condition, he would crawl out of the well into his tunnel in search of water. But the Y-shaped tunnel forked. The worm faced two choices. Now the observers would brightly light the well at the end of one branch of the fork and leave the other in darkness. If the worm chose the lighted well, the maze would be instantly flooded as a reward.

A training session for a worm consisted of ten or fifteen trials, and sessions were held every other day. To take account of any innate preference for light or dark, half of the worms were trained to seek the bright well for water, half the darkened. To eliminate any directional prejudices based on right and left, which well to be illuminated was determined by chance. At the first day's session all worms chose by chance; success or failure was fifty-fifty. But even at the second session preferences developed; those being trained to move toward light did so more often than toward dark; those being trained to move toward dark did so more often than toward light. By the third session – a speed of learning difficult to believe – most worms hit their peaks and chose correctly four times out of five. Then came out of nowhere the incredible collapse.

It is at this moment that we, like the observers, enter the haunted house of psychological beginnings. Almost without exception every planarian worm, once he attained a success of about 80 per cent, began choosing the wrong road in preference to the right. That he "knew" what he was doing was inarguable. Had he simply forgotten his lessons, he would have relapsed to the fifty-fifty original score, determined by chance. But he ·did not. He dropped to one out of three. He was discriminating *against* the right choice.

Best describes himself and his colleague as being appalled. They must have been. It is a great enough mystery that such a creature could learn anything. It is an accomplishment defying one's understanding that he could learn so rapidly. But that on the verge of total success the planarian worms should uniformly embrace perversity lies entirely beyond explanation. And to make matters worse, further trials brought rejection not only of the right answer, but of the experiment itself. When the maze went dry the worms curled up, refused to go anywhere, and in arrant rebellion opted for inevitable death in preference to further learning.

The harried investigators, faced by the organic equivalent of apples falling upward and straight lines turning corners, bumbled about trying to find means of appeasing their tiny rebels, who by now had taken charge of the experiment. Perhaps there was something about the kind of plastic used in molding the maze that made worms unhappy. They found other materials. The worms remained unmoved. Perhaps the mere threat of death in a drought was not enough and the worms were on strike for inexpressible fringe benefits. The scientists added that supreme planarian delicacy, finely chopped liver, to the water in the wells which they were supposed to crawl to. The worms remained adamant, muttering some planarian equivalent of "The hell with it." By this point in the experiment it was not the mentality of the worms being tested but the sanity of scientists, and hysteria hovered close by. When somebody wondered if the worms might be suffering from claustrophobia, hysteria seemed, in truth, to have closed in. Another maze was built. It offered not merely water-filled wells to save worm life but a new spaciousness at worm's end, a sense of freedom and elbow room where a worm could feel like a worm. And lo! it worked. It had been claustrophobia. The worms co-operated.

Any scientist in his right mind would with this climax assume that he had seen everything. But by now both Best and Rubinstein had long since lost touch with their right minds. They became infatuated with the possibility that worms who could suffer from claustrophobia might also have suffered boredom from a lesson so easily mastered. Fortunately for the future of psychology there was no one present to point out to the two mad scientists that a creature lacking proper brain, proper nervous system, proper belly, proper sex life, and even proper rectum has nothing under the sun to get bored with. Since no one was looking, they constructed another maze, an exact duplicate of the original, but made of rought plastic instead of smooth.

Now they started the experiment all over again. They used the smooth maze as before. They trained their worms to head for brightened or darkened wells, each as loaded with claustrophobia as the wells had been in the first place. Predictably, when the worms hit a level of 80 per cent success they promptly went into a decline and started choosing wrong answers. But now the scientists clapped them in the maze that would feel rough on their undersides as they crawled along. From that day on, half of the trials were conducted in the smooth maze, half the rough. A worm had to learn that if he felt smooth plastic against his undersides he must head for the light to reach water, but if he found himself crawling over rough plastic then to gain water he must head for the dark. In the testing of monkeys and children this is known as a double-ambiguity problem.

One out of every three planarian worms mastered the double-ambiguity problem. Sometimes when they reached the fork they would hesitate, pointing their heads first one way then the other, as if trying to make up their "minds." In animal study this is known as "vicarious trial-and-error behavior." Sometimes, unable to make up their "minds," they would go back to the starting point and begin again. But of the one out of every three who succeeded in mastering the whole problem, none ever grew bored again. None ever showed perversity, none ever rebelled, none ever curled up in tight defiance or muttered, grimly, the hell with it.

Where are we? What forces do we behold when we inspect the mind of worm or man? What is this everlasting scenery that graces our stages? What are these staircases that life has always climbed? What are these beds that life has always slept in, these antique furnishings that seem forever to have been life's own?

We do not know. Our ignorance of the human being is as massive and as measurable as our ignorance of the planarian worm. We are equivalent mysteries, and the man who says otherwise is the supreme ignoramus among us.'

bibliography

The literature suggested is not a comprehensive bibliography. It is to assist those who wish to study some of the basic reading in given fields.

A guide to organisational development

C. ARGYRIS, *Understanding Organisational Behaviour.* Tavistock Publications, 1960.

WARREN G. BENNIS, *Organizational Development – Its Nature, Origin and Prospect.* Addison Wesley, London, 1969.

RICHARD BECKHARD, *Organizational Development, Strategies and Models.* Addison Wesley, London, 1969.

ROBERT BLAKE AND J. S. MOUTAN, *Building a Dynamic Corporation through GRID Organisational Development.* Addison Wesley, London, 1969.

BURNS & STALKER, *The Management of Innovation.* Tavistock Publications Ltd.

R. H. GUEST, *Organisational Change.* Tavistock Publications, 1962.

A. C. HAZEL AND A. S. REID, *Enjoying a Profitable Business.* Business Books, 1971.

P. HILL, *Towards a New Philosophy of Management – A Study of the Company Development Programme at Shell UK.* Gower Press, 1971.

ALEX S. IRVINE, *Improving Industrial Communication* (Basic guide for line managers). Industrial Society, Gower Press, London, 1971.

R. KAHN, *et al, Organisational Stress; Studies in Role Conflict and Ambiguity.* J. Wiley & Sons, 1964.

PAUL R. LAWRENCE AND J. W. LORSCH, *Developing Organizations.* Addison Wesley, London, 1969.

E. J. MILLER AND A. K. RICE, *Systems of Organisation*. Tavistock Publications, 1970.

RACKHAM, HONEY AND COLBERT, *Developing Interactive Skills*. Wellens Publishing, 1972.

W. J. REDDIN, *Managerial Effectiveness*. McGraw-Hill, London.

D. SADLER AND B. BARRY, *Organisational Development*. Longmans, London, 1970.

EDGAR H. SCHEIN, *Process Consultation: Its Role in Organizational Development*. Addison Wesley, London, 1969.

EDGAR H. SCHEIN AND WARREN G. BENNIS, *Personal and Organisational Change through Group Methods*. J. Wiley & Sons, London, 1965.

REX WINSBURY, *Modern Japanese Management*. BIM, 1970.

A guide to selection and recruitment

E. ANSTEY, *Psychological Tests*. Nelson, 1966.

C. ARGYRIS, *Integrating the Individual and the Organization*. Wiley, 1964.

W. E. BEVERIDGE, *Problem Solving Interviews*. Allen & Unwin, 1968.

R. BORGER AND A. E. M. SEABORNE, *The Psychology of Learning*. Pelican, 1966.

BRITISH INSTITUTE OF MANAGEMENT, *Selection of Staff*. British Institute of Management, 1960.

E. DE BONO, *The Use of Lateral Thinking*. Jonathan Cape, 1967.

M. D. DUNNETTE, *Personnel Selection and Placement*. Tavistock Publications, 1966.

J. MUNRO FRASER, *Employment Interviewing* (4th Edition). Macdonald & Evans, 1966.

JOHN S. GOUGH, *Interviewing in Twenty-Six Steps*. BACIE, 1961.

E. HOPSON AND J. HAYES, *The Theory and Practice of Vocational Guidance*. Pergamon Press, 1969.

INDUSTRIAL SOCIETY, *A Guide to Employment Practices*. Industrial Society, London, 1970.

W. LAMB, *et al.*, *Management Behaviour*, Duckworth, 1969.

C. H. LAWSHE AND M. J. BALMA, *Principles of Personnel Testing*. McGraw-Hill, 1966.

M. M. MANDELL, *The Selection Process*. American Management Assoc., 1965.

NATIONAL INSTITUTE OF INDUSTRIAL PSYCHOLOGY, *The Seven-Point Plan*. NIIP.

E. SANDS, *How to Select Executive Personnel.* Chapman & Hall, 1963.

E. SIDNEY AND M. BROWN, *The Skills of Interviewing.* Tavistock Publications, 1961.

R. H. THOULESS, *Straight and Crooked Thinking.* Pan, 1963.

ROY VAN GELDER, *Induction.* Industrial Society, London, 1970.

P. E. VERNON, *Intelligence and Attainment Tests.* University of London Press, 1960.

A guide to job evaluation and merit rating

E. ANSTEY, *Staff Reporting and Staff Development.* Allen & Unwin, 1961.

BRITISH INSTITUTE OF MANAGEMENT, *Job Evaluation.* Management Publications, 1971.

J. DOULTON AND D. HAY, *Managerial and Professional Staff Grading.* Allen & Unwin, 1962.

A. FOX, *The Time Span of Discretion Theory: An Appraisal.* Institute of Personnel Management, London, 1966.

INDUSTRIAL SOCIETY, *Job Evaluation.* Industrial Society, 1970.

M. S. KELLOGG, *What to do about Performance Appraisal.* American Management Assoc., 1965.

J. WALKER MORRIS, *Job Evaluation.* Institute of Supervisory Management, 1966.

INSTITUTE OF OFFICE MANAGEMENT, *Clerical Job Grading and Merit Rating.* Institute of Office Management, London, 1960.

T. T. PATTERSON, *Job Evaluation.* Business Books, 1972. Volume 1: *A New Method;* Volume 2: *A Manual for the Patterson Method.*

H. E. ROFF AND T. E. WATSON, *Job Analysis.* Institute of Personnel Management, London, 1966.

TRADES UNION CONGRESS, *Job Evaluation and Merit Rating.* Trades Union Congress, 1964.

M. WILLIAMS, *Appraising Performance.* Institute of Supervisory Management, 1968.

A guide to wages, salaries and incentives

W. BROWN, *Piecework Abandoned.* Heinemann, 1962.

J. E. GENDERS AND N. J. URWIN, *Wages and Salaries.* Institute of Personnel Management, London, 1962.

Bibliography

INDUSTRIAL SOCIETY, *Cost of the Personnel Function*. Industrial Society, London, 1968.

E. JAQUES, *Progression Handbook*. Heinemann, 1968.

E. JAQUES, *Time-Span Handbook*. Heinemann, 1964.

F. E. LESIEUR (Ed.), *The Scanlon Plan*. John Wiley, 1959.

H. M. LEVINSON, *Determining Forces in Collective Wage Bargaining* (American). John Wiley, 1966.

H. LYDALL, *The Structure of Earnings*. Oxford University Press, 1968.

G. MCBEATH, *Management Remuneration Policy*. Business Books, 1969.

G. MCBEATH AND D. N. RANDS, *Salary Administration*. Business Publications, 1964.

A. J. MERRETT, *Executive Remuneration in the U.K.* Longmans Green, 1968.

A. J. MERRETT AND M. R. M. WHITE, *Incentive Payment Systems for Managers*. Gower Press, 1968.

D. T. B. NORTH AND G. L. BUCKINGHAM, *Productivity Agreements and Wage Systems*. Gower Press, 1969.

The Condemned Piecework – a study in Swedish industry, Swedish Employers' Federation, 1972.

A guide to employee motivation and job enrichment

C. ARGYRIS, *Integrating the Individual and the Organisation*. Wiley, London, 1964.

M. BROWN, *The Manager's Guide to the Behavioural Sciences*. Industrial Society, 1970.

R. H. CYERT AND J. G. MARCH, *A Behavioural Theory of the Firm*. Prentice-Hall, 1963.

P. DRUCKER, *The New Society*. Heinemann, 1951.

O. G. EDHOLM, *The Biology of Work*. Weidenfeld & Nicolson, London, 1967.

R. FORD, *Motivation through the Work Itself*. American Management Assoc., 1970.

S. W. GELLERMAN, *Management by Motivation*. American Management Assoc., 1968.

S. W. GELLERMAN, *Motivation and Productivity*. American Management Assoc., 1963.

M. HAIRE, *Psychology in Management*. McGraw-Hill, 1964.

Bibliography

F. HERZBERG, *et al.*, *The Motivation to Work*. Wiley, 1959.

F. HERZBERG, *Work and Nature of Man*. Staples Press, 1968.

P. HILL, *Towards a New Philosophy of Management – A Study of the Company Development Programme at Shell UK*. Gower Press, 1972.

INSTITUTE OF WORK STUDY PRACTITIONERS. *A Survey of Some Western European Experiments in Motivation*, 1971.

H. J. LEAVITT, *Managerial Psychology. An Introduction to Individuals and Groups in an Organisation*. Chicago University Press, 1964.

RENSIS LICKERT, *New Patterns of Management*. McGraw-Hill, 1961.

RENSIS LIKERT, *The Human Organization: Its Management and Value*. McGraw-Hill, 1967.

T. LUPTON, *Management and The Social Sciences*. Hutchinson, 1966.

ELTON MAYO, *The Human Problems of an Industrial Civilization*. Macmillan, 1933.

A. MASLOW, *Motivation and Personality*. Harper & Row, 1954.

D. MCGREGOR, *Leadership and Motivation*. M.I.T. Press, USA, 1968.

D. MCGREGOR, *The Human Side of Enterprise*. McGraw-Hill, 1960.

E. J. MILLER AND A. K. RICE, *Systems of Organization*. Tavistock Publications, 1967.

W. J. PAUL AND K. B. ROBERTSON, *Job Enrichment and Employee Motivation. Results of Large Scale Application of Job Enrichment in UK Industry*. Gower Press, 1970.

GORDON RATTRAM TAYLOR, *Rethink – a paraprimative solution*. Secker & Warburg, 1972.

EDGAR SCHEIN, *Organisational Psychology* (Foundation of Modern Psychology Series). Prentice-Hall Inc., 1965.

SHEPPARD AND HERRICK, *Where Have All the Robots Gone? Worker Dissatisfaction in the 70s*. Collier-MacMillan, 1972.

VICTOR H. VROOM, *Work and Motivation*. J. Wiley & Son, 1964.

MANECK S. WADIA, *Management and the Behavioural Sciences* (Text and Readings). Boston, Allyn & Bacon Inc., 1968.

REX WINSBURY, *Modern Japanese Management*. BIM, 1970.

Articles on employee motivation and job enrichment

A three-week series by STEPHEN ARIS on the techniques now sweeping UK boardrooms! 'The Games Managers Play' including UK companies experiences with The Management Grid, the theories of

Bibliography

FREDERICK HERZBERG, and the work of REDDIN, COVERDALE, *et al. Sunday Times*, 24th, 31st January and 7th February 1971.

RICHARD BECKHARD, 'Motivation through effective management'. Paper read to the British Institute of Management conference. *British Institute of Management*, 28th November 1967. London B.I.M. 1967.

P. F. DRUCKER, 'Management's new role'. *Harvard Business Review*, November/December 1969.

D. R. FRANCIS, 'Jobs fit for men'. *Management Today*, November 1968, p. 106.

JAY W. FORRESTER, 'Social structures and motivation for reducing research costs'. *Research Management*, January 1966, pp. 45–60.

HEINZ GOLDMAN, 'What motivates your salesmen?' *Marketing*, May 1967, pp. 249–251.

E. G. GOMERSALL AND M. SCOTT MYERS, 'Breakthrough in on-the-job-training'. *Harvard Business Review*, August 1966.

FREDERICK HERZBERG, 'One more time – How do you motivate employees'. *Harvard Business Review*, January/February 1968.

ROBERT J. HOUSE AND LAWRENCE A. WIGDOR, 'Herzberg's dual-factor theory of job satisfaction and motivation: a review of the evidence and a criticism'. *Personnel Psychology*, Winter 1967, pp. 369–389.

LYNDA KING TAYLOR, 'The manager's introduction to behavioural science'. *Management in Action*, London, February 1970.

LYNDA KING TAYLOR, 'Worker Participation in Sweden' (and associated articles). *Industrial and Commercial Training, 1973*.

DR. T. LUPTON, 'Methods of wage payment, organisational change and motivation'. *Work Study and Management*, December 1964, pp. 543–549.

DAVID C. MCLELLAND, 'The urge to achieve. Psychological research suggests that the will to get on can be isolated as a motive and taught'. *New Society*, 16th February 1967, pp. 227–229.

M. SCOTT MYERS, 'Who are your motivated workers?' *Harvard Business Review*, January/February 1964.

M. SCOTT MYERS, 'Conditions for manager motivation'. *Harvard Business Review*, January/February 1966.

DR. W. J. PAUL AND K. B. ROBERTSON, 'Job enrichment pays off'. An I.C.I. Report. *Harvard Business Review*, March 1969.

'Work structuring: a summary of experiments at N. V. Philips, Eindhoven, 1963–68'. *Philips-report*, 1969.

L. W. PORTER AND E. E. LAWLER III, 'What job attitudes tell about motivation'. *Harvard Business Review*, January/February 1968.

THEODORE V. PURCELL, 'Work psychology and business values: a triad theory of work motivation'. *Personnel Psychology*, Autumn 1967, pp. 231–257.

W. J. REDDIN, 'A 3-D development in management style theory'. *Journal of Institute of Personnel Management*, March 1967.

EDGAR H. SCHEIN, 'Attitude change during management education'. *Administrative Science Quarterly*, March 1967, pp. 601–628.

A guide to management by objectives

P. DRUCKER, *The Practice of Management* (Chapter 11: Management by objectives and self-control). Mercury Books (Heinemann), 1961.

A. FORREST, *The Manager's Guide to Setting Targets*. The Industrial Society, London, 1970.

S. GELLERMAN, *The Management of Human Relations* (Chapter 7: Performance appraisal and employee counselling). Holt, Rinehart & Winston, 1966.

J. HUMBLE, *Improving Management Performance*. British Institute of Management, 1966.

J. HUMBLE, *Management by Objectives in Action*. McGraw-Hill, London, 1970.

J. HUMBLE, *Improving Business Results*. McGraw-Hill, London, 1971.

M. W. B. KNIGHT, *Management by Objectives** (Smith's Industries–Electronics, etc.). Smiths Industries Ltd, 1966.

D. MCGREGOR, *The Human Side of Enterprise*. McGraw-Hill, 1960.

G. S. ODIORNE, *Management by Objectives: A System of Managerial Leadership*. Pitman, 1965.

W. J. REDDIN, *Effective MBO.** British Institute of Management, 1971.

Articles on management by objectives

G. CYRIAX, 'What kind of bonuses for management success?'. *Financial Times*, 4 May, 1967.

M. DIXON, 'An object lesson in business planning'* (Pilkington's: glass). *Guardian*, 16 November, 1967.

* Those articles and books marked thus * relate to MBO in specific industries or companies.

M. DIXON, 'Management by objectives sets the targets'* (Carborundum: abrasives and pottery). *Guardian*, 20 February, 1968.

A. M. DOWSON, 'Management by objectives'* (Hosiery Industry). *Hosiery Trade Journal*, February, 1967.

ELSBETH GANGUIN, 'Making biscuits with science'* (McVitie and Price: food). *Financial Times*, January, 1968.

ELSBETH, GANGUIN, 'Objectives in two firms'* (Quaker Oats: food; Yorkshire Imperial Metals: engineering). *Financial Times*, 12 January, 1968.

A. LUMSDEN, 'Clarifying the objectives'* (Viners: cutlery). *Management Today*, November, 1967.

D. E. P. OWEN, 'Setting objectives'. *Chartered Mechanical Engineer*, September, 1966.

K. ROWE, 'An appraisal of appraisals'. *Journal of Management Studies*, March, 1964.

M. WADE, 'Fine Fare – the management revival'* (Fine Fare: supermarkets). *Business Management*, December, 1967.

M. WADE, 'The only way to manage – far reaching effects of management by objectives'* (G.K.N.: engineering; Smith's Industries: electronics). *Business Management*, July, 1967.

A guide to creative thinking and decision making

DR. J. ADAIR, *Training for Leadership*. The Industrial Society, McDonald & Co, 1968.

R. R. BLAKE AND J. S. MOUTON, *Group Dynamics: Key to Decision Making*. Gulf Publishing Co, 1961.

R. R. BLAKE AND J. S. MOUTON, *The Managerial Grid-Key. Management Orientations for Obtaining Production through People*. University of Texas, 1962.

CHARLES R. BONINI, *Simulation of Information and Decision Systems in the Firm*. Prentice-Hall, 1963.

R. BURON, *Decision Making in the Development Field*. Paris, Organisation for Economic Co-operation and Development, 1966.

A. CROSBY, *Creativity and Performance in Industrial Organization*. Tavistock Publications, 1968.

EDWARD DE BONO, *Five Day Course in Thinking*. Allen Lane, Penguin Press, 1968.

Bibliography

EDWARD DE BONO, *Lateral Thinking for Management*. McGraw-Hill, London, 1970.

P. F. DRUCKER, *The Effective Executive*. Heinemann Ltd, 1967.

M. B. FOLSOM, *Executive Decision Making; Observations and Experience in Business and Government*. McGraw-Hill, 1962.

G. S. FULCHER, *Common Sense Decision Making*. Evenston, Northwestern University Press, 1965.

H. W. GABRIEL, *Technique of Creative Thinking for Management*. Prentice Hall, 1961.

J. R. GREENE AND R. L. SISSON, *Dynamic Management Decision Games*. Wiley, New York, 1959.

CARL E. GREGORY, *The Management of Intelligence: Scientific Solving and Creativity*. McGraw-Hill, 1967.

J. W. HAEFELE, *Creativity and Innovation*. Reinhold Publishing Co. (Chapman & Hall), 1962.

E. HODNETT, *The Art of Problem Solving: How to Improve Your Methods*. Harper, New York, 1955.

GARRY A. LUOMA, *Accounting Information in Managerial Decision-Making for Small and Medium Manufacturers*. National Association for Accountants, New York, 1967.

NORMAN R. F. MAIER, *Problem Solving; Discussions and Conferences; Leadership Methods and Skills*. McGraw-Hill, 1963.

SAMUEL J. MANTEL, *Cases in Managerial Decisions*. Prentice Hall, 1964.

J. S. MORGAN, *Improving Your Creativity on the Job*. American Management Association, New York, 1968.

H. A. SIMON, *Administrative Behaviour: A Study of Decision-Making Processes in Administrative Organization*. Macmillan, New York, 1957.

E. SMITH, *The Manager as an Action-Centred Leader*. The Industrial Society, London, 1970.

C. S. WHITING, *Creative Thinking*, Reinhold, New York, 1958.

REX WINSBURY, *Modern Japanese Management*. BIM, 1970.

A guide to employee participation

BRITISH INSTITUTE OF MANAGEMENT, *Industrial Democracy: Some Implications for Management* (Occasional Papers (New Series) OPN 1). British Institute of Management, 1968.

Bibliography

W. B. D. BROWN, *Exploration in Management*. Heinemann, 1962.

K. COATES AND A. TOPHAM, *Industrial Democracy in Great Britain*. MacGibbon & Kee, 1968.

P. DERRICK AND J. F. PHIPPS, *Co-ownership, Co-operation and Control: An Industrial Objective*. Longmans, 1969.

F. EMERY AND E. THORSRUD, *Industrial Democracy – Representation of Employees on the Boards of Companies*. Tavistock Publications, 1969.

A. FLANDERS, *et al, Experiment in Industrial Democracy: A Study of the John Lewis Partnership* (Society Today and Tomorrow). Faber & Faber, 1968.

S. W. GELLERMAN, *Management by Motivation*. American Management Association (Bailey Bros. & Swinfen), 1968.

F. HERZBERG, *Work and the Nature of Man*. Staples Press, 1970.

P. HILL, *Towards a New Philosophy of Management – A Study of the Company Development Programme at Shell UK*. Gower Press, 1971.

J. HENDERSON, *Effective Joint Consultation*. Industrial Society, 1970.

J. HENDERSON, *Examples of Joint Consultation*. Industrial Society, 1970.

INTERNATIONAL INSTITUTE FOR LABOUR STUDIES, 'Workers' participation in management'. *Bulletin 2*, February, 1967. IILS, Geneva, 1967.

ELLIOTT JAQUES, *The Changing Culture of a Factory: A Study of Authority and Participation in an Industrial Setting*. Tavistock Publications, 1951.

J. KELLY, *Is Scientific Management Possible?: A Critical Examination of Glacier's Theory of Organisation*. Faber & Faber, 1968.

LYNDA KING TAYLOR, 'Worker Participation in Sweden' (and associated articles). *Industrial and Commercial Training, 1973*.

THE LABOUR PARTY, *Industrial Democracy – Working Party Report*. Labour Party, 1967.

D. MCGREGOR, *The Human Side of Enterprise*. McGraw-Hill, 1960.

D. MCGREGOR, *The Professional Manager*. McGraw-Hill, 1967.

A. J. MARROW, *et al, Management by Participation*. Harper & Row, 1967.

W. J. PAUL AND K. B. ROBERTSON, *Job Enrichment and Employee Motivation*. Gower Press, 1970.

RACKHAM *et al., Developing Interactive Skills*. Wellens Publishing, 1971,

E. RHENMAN, *Industrial Democracy and Industrial Management: A Critical Essay on the Possible Meanings and Implications of Industrial Democracy*. Tavistock Publications, London, 1968.

R. SAWTELL, *Sharing Our Industrial Future*. Industrial Society, 1970.

W. H. SCOTT, *Industrial Leadership and Joint Consultation*. University of Liverpool Press, 1952.

A guide to retraining adult workers

E. BELBIN, 'Some studies of training older people'. *Age with a Future*, Munksgaard, Copenhagen, 1964.

R. M. BELBIN, 'Middle age: what happens to ability?'. *Middle Age*. BBC TV Publications, 1967. Ed. R. Owen.

E. BELBIN, 'A current problem in the middle aged: retraining in industry'. *Middle Age*. BBC TV Publications, 1967. Ed. R. Owen.

E. BELBIN AND R. M. BELBIN, 'Retraining and the older worker'. *Industrial Society: Social Science in Management*. Ed. D. Pym, Penguin, 1969.

R. M. BELBIN, 'The discovery method; an international experiment in retraining'. In the series *Employment of Older Workers*. OECD Paris, 1969.

R. M. BELBIN, 'Adults as learners; how do they learn?' *Teaching on Equal Terms*. J. Rogers. BBC, London, 1969.

E. BELBIN, 'Methods of training older workers'. Reprint in *Experimental Psychology in Industry*. Ed. D. Holding. Penguin Books Ltd, 1969.

R. MOTTRAM, 'Adults changing jobs: predicting trainability'. *Applied Gerontology*, 1 April, 1970.

D. B. NEWSHAM, 'The challenge of change to the adult trainee'. *Training Information*, Pamphlet No. 3, HMSO, 1969.

Articles on retraining adult workers

J. W. BARBER, 'Simulators and continued process operator training'. *BACIE Journal*, Vol. 19, pp. 11, 61–70, 1965.

E. BELBIN AND R. SERGEANT, 'The clothing industry in transition'. *Times Review of Industry and Technology*, 1964, pp. 2, 10, 40–42.

E. BELBIN AND S. SHIMMIN, 'Training the middle-aged for inspection work'. *Group Psychology*, 1964, pp. 38, 1, 49–57.

E. BELBIN, R. M. BELBIN AND S. DOWNS, 'Age and translation processes'. *Bulletin*, International Association of Applied Psychology, June 15, 1966, pp. 39–47.

E. BELBIN, 'Learning new skills in middle-age'. Central Office of Information *Newsletter*, Feature 2041/6, No. 8, August, 1966.

E. BELBIN AND P. WATERS, 'Organised home study for older retrainees' *Industrial Training International*, 2, pp. 196–198, 1967.

R. M. BELBIN, 'New possibilities in the retraining of older workers'. In *Solving the Problems of Retirement*, pp. 74–82, pub. Institute of Directors, 1968.

Bibliography

E. BELBIN AND R. M. BELBIN, 'Selecting and training adults for new work'. *Interdisciplinary Topics in Gerontology*, 4. Ed. A. T. Welford Basel: S. Karger, 1969, pp. 66–81.

R. M. BELBIN, 'The discovery method in training'. *Training Information* Pamphlet No. 5, HMSO, 1969.

R. M. BELBIN AND E. BELBIN, 'New careers in middle age'. In *Middle Age and Aging*. Ed. B. L. Neugarten. University of Chicago Press, 1969, pp. 341–346.

E. BELBIN AND M. H. TOYE, 'Adult learning. Forcing the pace'. *Applied Gerontology*, 1 April, 1970.

S. CHOWN, E. BELBIN AND S. DOWNS, 'Programmed instruction as a. method of teaching paired associates to older learners'. *Journal of Gerontology*, 22, pp. 212–219, 1967.

S. DOWNS, 'New skills in middle age'. *Personnel Management and Methods*, August, 1964, pp. 24–25.

S. DOWNS, 'Labour turnover in two public service organisations' *Occupational Psychology*, 41, pp. 137–142, 1967.

S. DOWNS, 'Selecting the older trainee'. NIIP *Bulletin*, pp. 19–26, May. 1968.

M. DIXON, 'Educate those older workers too'. *Guardian*, 9 July, 1968.

INDUSTRIAL TRAINING RESEARCH UNIT, 'Should older recruits be trained separately?' *Research Notes in Industrial and Commercial Training*. 1 December, 1969.

J. G. NEAYLE, M. H. TOYE AND E. BELBIN, 'Adult training: the use of programmed instruction'. *Occupational Psychology*, 42, pp. 23–31, 1968.

P. J. SOMMERFELD, 'Management training in Europe today. National and international organisations providing facilities'. *Works Management*, May, 1968, pp. 17–20, 1968.

M. H. TOYE, 'A rethink on basic skills'. *Industrial Training International*, 4, pp. 112–119, March, 1969.

A guide to industrial sociology and psychology

M. ARGYLE, et al., *Social Theory and Economic Change*. Tavistock Publications, 1967.

V. H. BRIX, *Cybernetics and Everyday Affairs*. D. Rendel, 1968.

T. BURNS AND G. M. STALKER, *The Management of Innovation*. Tavistock Publications, 1961.

P. F. DRUCKER, *The Landmarks of Tomorrow*. Heinemann, 1959.

P. F. DRUCKER, *New Markets and other Essays*. Heinemann, 1971.

148

Bibliography

T. EVANS AND M. STEWART, *Pathway to Tomorrow. The Impact of Automation on People.* Pergamon Press, 1967.

J. K. GALBRAITH, *The Affluent Society.* Hamish Hamilton, 1958.

J. H. GOLDTHORPE, et al, *The Affluent Worker: Industrial Attitudes and Behaviour.* Cambridge University Press.

ERIC HOFFER, *The True Believer.* Time Inc. Book Division, New York. 1963.

ELTON MAYO, *The Social Problems of an Industrial Civilisation.* Routledge & Kegan Paul, 1952.

R. MORRIS, *The Economics of Capital Utilisation. A Report on Multiple-Shift Work.* Cambridge University Press, 1964.

E. MUMFORD AND O. BANKS, *The Computer and the Clerk.* Routledge & Kegan Paul, 1967.

O.E.C.D., *Reviews of Manpower and Social Policies: the UK.* Paris, 1970 ›

S. R. PARKER, R. K. BROWN, J. CHILD AND M. A. SMITH, *The Sociology of Industry.* Allen & Unwin, 1967.

GORDON RATTRAY TAYLOR, *Rethink – a paraprimative solution.* Secker & Warburg, 1972.

A. SAMPSON, *New Anatomy of Britain.* Hodder & Stoughton, 1971.

A. SAMPSON, *The New Europeans.* Hodder & Stoughton, 1968.

M. SHANKS, *The Innovators.* Penguin, 1967.

RICHARD M. TITMUS, *Income Distribution and Social Change.* Allen & Unwin, 1962.

W. THORNHILL, *The Nationalized Industries.* Nelson, 1968.

C. WILSON, *New Pathways in Psychology – Maslow and the Post Freudian Revolution.* Gollancz, 1972.

Commuter reading

As promised in the first section of the book, I am enclosing in the appendix a light and at times satirical reading list for the commuter manager. The books share the dual advantage that they can be read for edification as well as for pleasure.

ROBERT ARDREY, *The Territorial Imperative.* Collins, 1967.

ARNOLD BENNET, 'How to live on 24 hours a day' (Essay).

ERIC BERNE, *Games People Play (Psychology of Human Relationships).* Andre Deutsch, 1967.

DARRELL HUFF, *How to lie with Statistics.* Victor Gollancz Ltd.

Bibliography

ANTHONY JAY, *Management and Machiaevelli*. Hodder & Stoughton, 1967. Penguin, 1970.

R. LINDHOLM, *The Perfect Factory*. Swedish Employers' Federation, 1972.

DESMOND MORRIS, *The Human Zoo*. Jonathan Cape.

DESMOND MORRIS, *The Naked Ape*. Jonathan Cape.

C. NORTHCOTE PARKINSON, *The Law of Delay*.

PEMBERTSON ADVERTISING AGENCY. *How to get the Better of Business*.

LAURENCE PETER (Raymond Hull, Professor of Education, University of South California), *The Peter Principle*. Souvenir Press.

LORD ROBENS, *Human Engineering*, Jonathan Cape, 1970.

GEOFFREY STUTTARD-MACDONALD, *Work is Hell*. University of London.

MARK SPADE, *How to run a Bassoon Factory* Hamish Hamilton.

MARK SPADE, *Business for Pleasure*. Hamish Hamilton.

ROBERT TOWNEND, *Up the Organization*. Michael Joseph.

ERIC WEBSTER, *How to win the Business Battle*. John Murray.

index

Institute of Personnel Management, 28
Institute of Work Study Practitioners, 94
Involvement, 30–1: downward and upward consultation, 30, 31

Jensen Motor Company, 114
Jephcott, Pearl, 7–8, 23
Job description, 71
Job enrichment, 28–9, 40, 43, 46, 48, 63–4, 67–72, 80–3, 87–8, 90, 100
Job satisfaction, 12–13, 90, 97
Johnson, Stephen, 74

Labour turnover, 16, 115–17
Leiding, Rudolf, 103
Lembke, Hans Herbert, 101
Lenin, quoted, 34
Linklater, Peter, 51

Maletz, Rudi, 101
Manpower in future, 27–30: experience of participation, 28; number of school leavers, 27
Marchont, Anthony, 74
Marlow Association, 19
Material security and satisfaction, 5–6, 12
Mercury House Group case study, 65–73; organisation of Group, 66; smallness of departments, 66; formal training function, 66; clerical and secretarial staff and wastage, 66–7; management training needs analysis, 67; study of job enrichment theory, 67; practical exercises, 67–8; training, 68–72; new responsibility and increased skills for secretaries, 68–70; upward and downward communication, 70; reduction in wastage, 72, 73; specimen job description, 71

Motivation, 29, 72; chart, 31, 32; needs, 4–6
Motivation and Productivity film series (BNA), 40

National Coal Board, 15–16
Needs, hierarchy of, 4–5
New Statesman and Nation, 7
Newton, John, 20, 23
Nordhoff, Professor Heinz, 103, 112

O & M techniques, 95, 99
Off Sick, Office of Health Economics pamphlet, 14, 15
Office staff turnover problems, 46–8
Owen Report, 18

Participation, 28, 30, 43, 55–7, 62, 80, 82, 83, 97–8
Paternalism, 81, 103
Payment-by-results systems, 76
Physiological needs, 4
Porsche, Ferdinand, 108, 112
Primary groups, 11–12

Responsibility, 30
Rice, D. P., 14
Robens, Lord, on absenteeism, 15–16

Safety needs, 4, 7
Schlipper, Herbert, 101
Secondary groups, 11, 12
Secretarial staff, 67–73: and job enrichment, 68–70; training, 68–72; wastage, 66–7
Security: of employment, 7; of income, 5–6; of information, 6
Selection for jobs, 89–90
Self-actualisation, 4, 5

Shell UK Ltd., case study
(Stanlow Refinery), 12, 51–64;
discussion of philosophy and
objectives, 52; reorganisation
of duties, 53; technical problems, 53; social system within
plant, 54; poor morale, 54;
weekly departmental meetings,
54–5; participative style of
management, 55–7, 62; flexibility, 55–7; abolition of
clocking, 56; relief cover
system, 56; recording of information, 56–7, 59–60; financial
control procedure, 58; involvement of operators in running
plant, 58–60; education and
training, 60; response, 60–2;
improved individual performance, 63; productivity deal, 63
Shop stewards, 20–1, 35, 104–5,
107
Sickness absence, 14–15, 20
Siemsens, Reimer, 101
Smith, Ian C., 33
Stein, Philip, 101
Strikes, 103, 107
*Survey of Western European
Experiments in Motivation*, 94
Swedish State Power Board case
study, 94–100; O & M group
and techniques, 95, 99; buyers
in head office purchasing
department, 95–100; original
hierarchical structure, 95; work
flow problem, 95–6; installation
of planning and objectives
system, 96; reorganised
structure, 96–7; attitude survey, 97; discovery of low job
satisfaction, 97, 99–100; further
participative review, 97–100;
further change and final
structure, 98–9; benefits and
expected results, 99

Target setting, 30

Tatton (William) and Co. Ltd.,
74–83
Tavistock Institute of Human
Relations, 52
Taylor's principle of scientific
'work study' management, 75–6
Territorial Imperative, The
(Ardrey), 119–22
Trade Unions, 19–21; mergers, 17
Trades Union Congress (TUC),
20
Training, 6, 29–30, 36, 40, 66,
89: for future growth, 6–7;
on-the-job courses, 40;
secretarial training, 68

Undergraduates' attitudes
towards industry, 9–10, 23, 81
'Unreachables', 28–9
'Untouchables', 29

Volkswagen case study, 19, 101–
12, 114; post-war history and
growth, 102–3; production
figures, 102; Beetle car, 102,
107–8, 112; industrial peace,
103–5; communication
system, 104; full time union
officials, 104, 107; shop
stewards, 104–5, 107; Works
Council (Betriebsrat), 104–8,
111; grievance procedures,
104; briefing system, 105, 106;
pay system, 107; German law
on strikes, 107; automation,
109–10; role of supervisors,
110; inspection methods, 110–
11; British market, 112
Volvo, research into boredom and
fatigue at work, 113–14

Walsh, William, 84
Watford Launderers and Cleaners,
and recognition and identity
for employees, 115